Managing Stress and Conflict in Libraries

Sheila Pantry OBE

facet publishing

© Sheila Pantry 2007

Published by Facet Publishing
7 Ridgmount Street, London WC1E 7AE

Except as otherwise permitted under the Copyright
Designs and Patents Act 1988 this publication may only be
reproduced, stored or transmitted in any form or by any
means, with the prior permission of the publisher, or, in
the case of reprographic reproduction, in accordance with
the terms of a licence issued by The Copyright Licensing
Agency. Enquiries concerning reproduction outside those
terms should be sent to Facet Publishing, 7 Ridgmount
Street, London WC1E 7AE.

British Library Cataloguing in Publication Data
A catalogue record for this book is available from the
British Library

ISBN 978-1-85604-613-8

First published 2007
Reprinted 2008

Typeset in 11/15pt Baskerville and Nimbus Sans by Facet
Publishing.
Printed and made in Great Britain by Cromwell Press Ltd,
Trowbridge, Wiltshire.

Contents

Acknowledgements

I appreciate the help given to me while compiling this book: from the staff of Facet Publishing, CILIP members who have given me their stories, and other colleagues who discussed various situations in their workplaces.

In particular, I thank my husband for reading the script and listening to my ideas during the writing.

My fervent hope is that all future workplaces will be safe, healthy and less stressful.

Glossary

ACAS	Advisory, Conciliation and Arbitration Service
BCS	British Crime Survey
CBI	Confederation of British Industry
CIPD	Chartered Institute of Personnel and Development
CISDOC	International Labour Office Health and Safety Centre's database
COSHH	Control of Substances Hazardous to Health Regulations
EC	European Commission
EU	European Union
HASAWA	The Health and Safety at Work etc. Act 1974
HSC	Health and Safety Commission
HSE	Health and Safety Executive
HSELINE	Health and Safety Executive Information Services database
ILO	International Labour Office (in Geneva)
MHSW	The Management of Health and Safety Regulations 1992
NIOSH	National Institute of Occupational Safety and Health (in USA)
NIOSHTIC	National Institute of Occupational Safety and Health databases
OPSI	Office of Public Sector Information
OSH	Occupational Safety and Health
RIDDOR	Reporting of Injuries, Diseases and Dangerous Occurrences Regulations 1995
TUC	Trades Union Congress
WRV	work-related violence

Introduction

Stress and conflict in the workplace undermine performance and can make people mentally and physically ill. Research indicates that ever-increasing numbers of people are experiencing excessive pressure of this kind in our rapidly changing world of work.

This applies to libraries and information organizations as much as anywhere; indeed they can be particular targets for verbal and non-verbal violent behaviour through their accessibility to the public. In addition, as in all organizations, a certain proportion of library staff is suffering aggression, abuse, bullying or harassment from a work colleague.

This book is written in response to this situation from the viewpoint of health and safety at work practice. Although people's ideas of standards of acceptable behaviour are likely to differ, it is vital that consensus is reached in each workplace.

Tackling – and preventing – conflict and stress effectively is a responsibility for management under health and safety legislation in the UK and many other countries. This can result in significant benefits for the organization in terms of recruitment and retention, employee commitment, performance and productivity, customer satisfaction, organizational image and reputation, and avoidance of potential litigation.

The book defines clearly what should and should not be tolerated in a healthy and safe working environment, and introduces the reporting procedures and communication skills essential in conflict resolution, enabling both employees and managers to consider situations consistently based on risk assessment previously carried out.

Chapter 1 looks at current health and safety concerns worldwide in the context of the fast moving world of work. It argues that employers must take a lead by producing guidelines and policies to bring about a conflict-free workplace. Chapter 2 looks at stress and conflict in the context of library and information organizations. It advocates that steps should be taken to ensure that everyone involved should clearly understand what is meant by the terms 'aggression', 'bullying', 'conflict', 'harassment', 'stress' and 'violence'. Importantly, this chapter helps you to decide if there is a problem and to understand how such behaviour can affect people physically and mentally.

The business case is presented in Chapter 3. As well as endorsing the benefits of stress and conflict management, it also includes advice on the management of change: keeping staff involved and informed; dealing with internal conflict, managerial pressure and external pressures (e.g. outsourcing, downsizing); and ensuring employee commitment to work and management commitment to staff.

Chapter 4 introduces the five steps of a risk assessment and emphasizes the necessity of carrying one out, with the legal responsibilities involved. Chapter 5 further demonstrates how a risk assessment should be carried out: what happens at each step, and, once an overall picture has been obtained, the reasons why management must accept responsibility for any problems that are identified.

Chapter 6 offers organizational guidance and resources from the UK, Europe and worldwide, as well as recommending sources of advice on preventative measures that are currently in use.

Chapter 7 gives practical advice on preventative measures, and also outlines the steps to take if you find you are at risk; whilst Chapter 8 advises on how to react when faced with aggression and violence. It outlines personal safety measures that can be taken – especially while working alone or on the move – and stresses the vital role of effective communication skills. It also covers self-defence, dealing with physical attacks, and what to do in the aftermath of an incident. Finally, the very important issue of health and safety training is discussed; because all workplaces change with time it is vital to be aware that refresher training should be arranged regularly. The chapter identifies essential requirements for training, networking and counselling provision in the workplace.

A victim will need help both inside and outside the organization, and

Chapter 9 covers the support to be expected, whether immediate or long-term, after an incident.

The title of Chapter 10 is 'You are not Alone', and sadly these stories sent in response to an appeal in CILIP's *Library + Information Gazette* are real-life cases of aggression and violence that have been experienced, and in some cases are still being experienced, in our own profession. What an indictment! Work should be rewarding and fun – not stressful and harmful as these studies show.

The Appendices offer sources of further information including literature, support organizations, databases, websites and relevant legislation.

This book is essential reading for LIS employees at all levels, and also for managers, team leaders, supervisors, personnel and human resources staff, complaints officers, union officers and anyone else in the information organization who may be called upon to deal with people.

Sheila Pantry OBE

1 Current concerns worldwide

A worldwide problem

Unfortunately, aggression, bullying, conflict, harassment and violence in the workplace are not new, and neither are they decreasing. Pressure is part and parcel of all work and helps to keep us motivated. But excessive pressure and other forms of aggression, bullying and conflict can lead to violence – all of which undermines performance, is costly to employers and can make people ill.

Some governments and organizations worldwide have tried, particularly over the past 10 years, to try and contain these problems – by legislation, guidance and advice.

The information and references in this book will help you to understand the causes, and to identify and solve problems in your workplace.

The changing world of work

In 2005, the International Labour Office in Geneva commissioned a report entitled *The Cost of Violence/Stress at Work and the Benefits of a Violence/Stress-Free Working Environment* (Hoel, Sparks and Cooper, 2005). The results show that stress is an increasing workplace phenomenon negatively affecting a growing number of people across the world.

As the economy becomes global and competition increases in the battle for market share and survival, pressure mounts on workers. With high levels of crime and aggression in society, violence finds its way into the workplace in the form of robbery and assaults, particularly on frontline staff and service providers such as those in our libraries and information centres. As pressures mount, aggression may also build up *within* the workplace, making worker on worker aggression more likely. Recent research in Europe, the USA and Australia indicates that it is the emotional and psychological abuse referred to as 'bullying' and 'mobbing', rather than physical violence, which represents the greatest threat to most workers. However, due to the increasing diversity of workforces, a number of studies also document the frequent presence of harassment on the basis of race or gender. Additionally, many women, particularly in the developing world, have found that the workplace represents no safe haven from abusers.

Listed below are some current factors and trends which may affect the presence and scale of stress and violence:

- Economically, we are moving towards a single, global marketplace.
- There is increased commercial competition, which results in growing pressures on everyone at work.
- Survival in this competitive environment is not assured; organizations are restructuring and downsizing with the aim of cutting costs.
- Tendering for contracts has become increasingly common in the public sector, bringing with it more economic risk-taking in order to reduce cost.
- Outsourcing of jobs creates anxiety for current jobholders.
- Downsizing and restructuring has resulted in greater pressure on remaining employees, with an increase in their workload and workpace.
- Such intensification of work has resulted in employees (e.g. in the USA and the UK) working longer hours.

■ More short-term contract work, temporary and part-time work increases tensions in the workplace.

■ Perceptions of job insecurity generally are increasing in the industrialized world (there is no such thing now as a cradle-to-grave job).

The following global trends will also have an increasing effect:

■ In many countries it is the service sector, including libraries and information services, that is increasing most rapidly, with growing demands and pressure from clients and customers affecting the well-being of the staff.

■ The revolution in computing and telecommunications is gradually transforming work processes. A greater number of workers are being employed in teleworking, with their private home being their workplace.

■ With this wider definition of 'workplace' has come a need for new measures to ensure that basic health and safety regulations are applied at home.

■ The organization of work is changing, with more people working in self-directed or autonomous teams, etc.

■ In many countries the workforce is diversifying. This diversity may refer to gender, race, physical ability and/or sexual orientation. Where such development is not managed properly it may give rise to tension and conflict among groups of employees.

Research and legislation

The British Crime Survey (BCS) is a large, nationally representative household survey which measures the extent and nature of crimes committed against people living in England and Wales. Each sweep of the survey asks respondents about their experiences of criminal victimization in the previous year.

The BCS provides the most comprehensive and reliable findings to date on the extent and nature of violence at work in England and Wales. The large representative sample and the continuity of questions between sweeps mean that the BCS is uniquely placed to examine violence at work at the national level. The BCS has a sufficiently large sample (by combining several sweeps of the survey) to examine the nature of violence at work, and how risks of violence at work vary among different occupational groups.

During the 1980s and 1990s, violence at work began to attract increasing media attention. High profile incidents of violence at work have been reported in the media and have raised awareness of the issue among the public, employers, trade unions and the government. The Health and Safety Executive, the UK government agency with responsibility for advising on violence at work, has been producing guidelines on its prevention since the mid-1980s.

Legislation has also been introduced which recognizes violence at work as a health and safety issue. Since 1995, the Reporting of Injuries, Diseases and Dangerous Occurrences Regulations (RIDDOR) have required employers to report to their enforcing authority (usually the HSE or their local authority, depending on the type of premises) acts of physical violence which cause a fatality, a major injury or someone's absence from their normal work for more than three days.

The Protection from Harassment Act 1997 states:

(1) A person must not pursue a course of conduct – a) which amounts to harassment of another, and b) which he knows or ought to know amounts to harassment of the other. (2) For the purposes of this section, the person whose course of conduct is in question ought to know that it amounts to harassment of another if a reasonable person in possession of the same information would think the course of conduct amounted to harassment of the other.

There are also other pieces of legislation, which will be discussed later in this book.

There has also been an increasing amount of academic research into violence at work. The main thrust of this research has been to identify the extent and nature of the problem, and thus inform strategies for its prevention.

Definitions of violence, stress and harassment at work

Definitions of violence form a continuum ranging from physical assault to broader definitions which also include threat, intimidation, verbal abuse and emotional or psychological abuse. Those who favour the inclusion of non-physical acts in the definition of violence argue that the consequences of non-physical and physical violence may be equally serious.

Apart from the problem of defining violence generally, there are additional issues with defining violence at work. Some commentators restrict violence at work to those incidents in which the offender is a member of the public, while others also include incidents between work colleagues. There is also debate about whether to restrict the definition to 'workplace' violence (i.e. only incidents that occur at the workplace) or widen it to include all incidents related to work regardless of where they occur (the term 'work-related violence' is often used in this sense).

Although flexibility in defining the problem is useful, as the most appropriate definition may vary across different contexts, a single overarching definition that recognizes the continuum of behaviours that constitute violence is important in defining the problem at a national level.

CILIP

The definition of The Library Association (CILIP's predecessor) as far back as 1987 was:

> the term 'violence in libraries' can be seen as shorthand for describing all sorts of anti-social behaviour, ranging from spitting, damaging furniture or playing radios, to theft, verbal abuse and physical attack.
>
> (Library Association, 1987)

European Commission

The following definition has been adopted by the European Commission:

Incidents where persons are abused, threatened or assaulted in circumstances related to their work, involving an explicit or implicit challenge to their safety, well-being or health.

Health and Safety Executive (HSE)

The definition of violence at work adopted by the HSE is as follows:

Any incident in which an individual suffers verbal abuse, physical abuse or threats in circumstances relating to their work.

Also, the HSE defines work-related stress as

The adverse reaction people have to excessive pressure or other types of demand placed on them.

The British Crime Survey (BCS)

The BCS measures both physical assaults and threats, and therefore provides a relatively broad definition of violence at work. The definition of violence at work used in BCS reports is as follows:

All assaults or threats which occurred while the victim was working and were perpetrated by members of the public. Physical assaults include the offences of common assault, wounding, robbery and snatch theft. Threats include both verbal threats, made to or against the respondent, and non-verbal intimidation. They are mainly threats to assault the victim, though some threats relate to damaging property. The term violence is used in the BCS reports to refer to both assaults and threats. Members of the public include clients or customers previously known to the victim, people the victim did not know before the incident (usually customers or clients), friends, neighbours and local children.

Swedish National Board of Occupational Safety and Health

The Swedish National Board of Occupational Safety and Health defines the problem as:

> recurrent reprehensible or distinctly negative actions which are directed against individual employees in an offensive manner and can result in those employees being placed outside the workplace community.

The European Agency for Health and Safety at Work

The Agency's Fact Sheet 23 states:

> Workplace bullying is repeated, unreasonable behaviour directed towards an employee, or group of employees, that creates a risk to health and safety.

Within this definition, 'unreasonable behaviour' means behaviour that a reasonable person, having regard to all the circumstances, would expect to victimize, humiliate, undermine or threaten. 'Behaviour' includes the actions of individuals or of a group. A system of work may be used as a means of victimizing, humiliating, undermining or threatening. 'Risk to health and safety' includes risk to the mental or physical health of the employee. Bullying often involves a misuse or abuse of power, where the targets can experience difficulties in defending themselves.

The Advisory, Conciliation and Arbitration Service

In general terms, ACAS defines harassment as:

> unwanted conduct affecting the dignity of men and women in the workplace. It may be related to age, sex, race, disability, religion, nationality or any personal characteristic of the individual, and may be persistent or an isolated incident. The key is that the actions or comments are viewed as demeaning and unacceptable to the recipient.

Harassment can also have a specific meaning under certain laws (for instance if harassment is related to sex, race or disability, it may be unlawful discrimination). From December 2003 the UK law also gives protection against harassment relating to religion or belief and sexual orientation.

Costs of workplace stress and bullying

According to the Confederation of British Industry (CBI), stress now costs the UK over £12 billion a year, and employers £495 a year in direct costs for every worker employed. Indirect costs are probably considerably more (CBI, 2007).

The HSE estimates that bullying costs employers 80 million working days and up to £2 billion in lost revenue every year. Nearly half a million people in Britain experience work-related stress at a level they believe is making them ill, and the financial costs to society are estimated at £3.8 billion a year (see the HSE website at www.hse.gov.uk/stress/research.htm).

The mental and emotional scars may, in some cases, last a very long time: – see, for example, some of the cases quoted in Chapter 10 'You are not Alone'.

Tackling the problem

According to a recent study entitled *Bullying at Work: beyond policies to a culture of respect*, by the Chartered Institute of Personnel and Development (CIPD, 2006a), bullying in the workplace is frequently swept under the carpet by employers, mainly because managers do not have the skills to tackle the problem. This CIPD study aims to tackle bullying at work, placing an emphasis on:

■ defining the positive behaviours we can all expect from each other
■ everyone accepting responsibility for their behaviour and actions
■ everyone accepting responsibility for finding solutions
■ 'top team' behaviour, which is vital in reinforcing positive behaviours and creating a culture that goes beyond paying lip service to fairness.

Being clear about people's roles, communicating consistently and effectively, understanding expectations and being given what you need to do your job – all these are also destinations on a new route forward in tackling bullying at work.

HSE's report *Bullying at Work: a review of the literature* (HSE, 2006b) states that before discussing a definition of bullying at work, people should consider behaviours that are often confused with and have been used to justify bullying at work. These include terms such as 'strong management', 'tough management', 'assertiveness', etc. It is suggested that the use of bullying as a management tool is a clear indication of poor management practice. It is clear from the figures in this report that bullied employees are unlikely to be operating at their maximum level of productivity. They are unfortunately more likely to be suffering psychological stress, and possibly to be absent from work.

There is also the negative impact upon those employees who witness bullying within the workplace to take into consideration. Those who witness bullying are unlikely to have a positive view of an organization that permits such behaviour to continue.

Employers need to demonstrate what they are doing

Employers need to be able to show evidence that they are taking steps to look after their employees – Section 2 of the Health and Safety at Work etc. Act 1974 gives employers a duty of care to their staff and the public, and the Management of Health and Safety at Work Regulations 1992 require employers to undertake risk assessment, which includes risk of violence. The revised Reporting of Injuries, Diseases and Dangerous Occurrences Regulations (RIDDOR) 1995 specifically requires workplace violence to be reported. You should be aware that aggression and violence could take place between employees, or between employees and managers.

Ignorance of the law is no excuse, so employers in all information industry sectors – higher education, public and private sectors – need to be up-to-date with their knowledge of the latest legal requirements. If these employers think that libraries and information centres are nice quiet backwaters they should take a 'management by walking about' approach, on a regular basis, and spend time talking to those working in the various sections and departments to see what is actually happening.

Tackling the problem worldwide

Aggression, bullying, conflict, harassment, stress and violence at work are not unique to the UK: a survey of the major occupational health and safety databases in the OSH UPDATE service (www.oshupdate.com, which includes HSELINE from the UK's Health and Safety Executive Information Services, CISDOC from the International Labour Office Health and Safety Centre, the European Agency for Safety and Health at Work list of publications, and NIOSHTIC and NIOSHTIC-2 from the USA's National Institute of Occupational Safety and Health) reveals growing concern over workplace violence around the world. In particular, the literature shows that authorities and organizations in Australia, Canada, the wider European Union, New Zealand, South Africa and the USA have already recognized the problems and are taking action.

Results of a UK anti-bullying project

The findings from the world's largest anti-workplace bullying joint research project by Amicus and the UK Department of Trade and Industry (DTI) – the 'Dignity at Work Partnership' – were revealed on 2 October 2006.

In a poll conducted by Amicus, as part of the project, it was found that only 2% of employers took a zero tolerance approach to bullying. A huge 97% of organizations had never quantified the impact of bullying. And 80% of organizations had an anti-bullying policy in place but, despite this, more than half of those polled still thought bullying was an issue in their organizations.

The key finding in the research project (conducted by Portsmouth University) was that organizations who took a zero tolerance approach were the organizations who dealt with the problem most effectively.

The project addressed the serious issue of bullying in the workplace, which is estimated to cost UK employers over £2 billion a year in sick pay, staff turnover and loss of production. One in 10 employees say they have been bullied. The research project gives a contemporary view of good practice in dealing with bullying and harassment, and how the problem is dealt with in the workplace. The recommendations of the project include:

■ A zero tolerance approach should be adopted.
■ In partnership with unions, organizations must encourage consultation with employees on early intervention strategies.
■ It should be recognized that bullying is an organizational issue rather than simply a problem between individuals.
■ All anti-bullying and harassment policies should be clearly set out and communicated, along with the business case for doing so.
■ Organizations should use the term 'bullying' to describe negative behaviours.
■ All managers should be trained in mediation and conflict resolution skills.
■ Managers at the very top should lead by good example and a senior member of management should become the 'anti-bullying champion'.

Amicus General Secretary, Derek Simpson, said:

Bullying in the workplace can destroy people's lives. Our project aims to tackle this problem in partnership with employers by taking a zero tolerance approach to bullying from the outset.

Trade and Industry Secretary, Alistair Darling, said:

Bullying at work is a big problem and employers need to be aware of it. It corrodes employees' self-confidence and self-esteem and leads to a hostile working environment. It's bad for staff and it's bad for business.

People who feel harassed or victimised cannot do their job properly. And businesses that do not tackle bullying suffer from days lost through stress and illness, decreased productivity and damage to their reputation.

The Dignity At Work report gives businesses and organizations the tools they need to make zero-tolerance of bullying a reality for all workers.

Key to the findings is that policies alone will not secure a harassment-free working environment. Employees need to be involved in creating and implementing initiatives, which leads to ownership both of the problem and the solution.

So, employers need to agree with employees an acceptable level of behaviour in their organizations, and make sure that everyone understands the definitions clearly.

You will find more on preventative measures in later chapters.

POINTS TO REFLECT ON . . .

■ Do you think there is a problem with aggression, bullying, conflict and violence in your workplace?

■ Do you understand the effects of these problems on the individual?

■ If, after checking, there is not enough evidence, remember that you could check again at a later stage.

■ Do you have enough evidence and information to discuss the problem with colleagues and managers?

2 Are you at risk?

In this chapter you will find information on:

- why information centres and libraries are targets
- the causes of aggression and other work-related problems in information centres and libraries
- what is meant by aggression, bullying, conflict, harassment, stress and violence
- whose concern the problem is
- being constantly alert
- understanding how such behaviour can affect you physically and mentally
- making sure you are safe
- deciding if there is a problem
- first steps to take
- what to record and how to classify.

Since the mid-1990s the whole scene has moved on as far as aggression, bullying (verbal and non-verbal), conflict and physical violence in the workplace is concerned – people have more legal protection and certainly many know their rights, but there is still a lack of management intervention in many workplaces.

Why information centres and libraries?

Information centres and libraries tend to be places that are easily accessible, warm, informal and welcoming – it goes with the ethos of helping people to find information. As far back as June 1987 The Library Association (CILIP's predecessor), in its pamphlet *Violence in Libraries: preventing aggressive and unacceptable behaviour in libraries* (Library Association, 1987), stated:

> The success of the service (offered to customers) very often depends on these attributes – but this same openness can mean that staff are vulnerable in the face of anti-social behaviour. It is important not to lose sight of the positive aspects of library and information services when considering the subject of violence, but nevertheless forward planning and good management practices can avoid or alleviate situations where staff find themselves in danger, or afraid or unable to cope.

What are the causes?

There are many reasons why aggression occurs in libraries or information centres. Easy access, long opening hours and friendly, helpful staff all contribute to making libraries and information centres seem welcoming and attractive places to visit. But this in itself can mean that staff are vulnerable, as acts of aggression and violence or generally anti-social behaviour can erupt without warning in today's violent society. Increased pressures on the workforce to improve productivity, de-layering of staff and financial cut-backs resulting in reduced staff numbers – all can contribute to an increase in aggression among both staff and customers. The following also cause problems:

- antagonistic behaviour by customers who oppose any authoritative regime, e.g.: restrictions on the number of books which can be borrowed at any one time, imposing a fine for late return of the books or calling closing time when the customer wants to stay longer
- lack of respect for others and their points of view
- excessive or inflexible workloads and demands on people
- targets not clearly defined, or impossible deadlines

■ poor working relationships and conflict between individuals, including possibly sexual or racial harassment
■ no clear code of policy or conduct
■ organizational change and uncertainty
■ styles of management and supervision which may encourage aggressive behaviour in the mistaken belief that it is 'strong' management
■ one section trying to get work from another section in order to survive.

It is also possible that aggressive behaviour between individuals and groups could be caused by the physical conditions of the working environment, such as excessive noise, vibration, heat or humidity, or other obvious workplace hazards which might not be adequately controlled.

What counts as aggressive and abusive behaviour?

The various forms of bullying can often be hard to recognize – they may not be obvious to others, and may be insidious. The recipient may think, 'Perhaps this is normal behaviour in this organization'. Some people may be anxious that others will consider them weak, or not up to the job, if they find the actions of others intimidating. They may be accused of 'over-reacting', and worry that they will not be believed if they do report incidents. Sometimes those being subjected to bullying or harassment appear to overreact to something that seems relatively trivial, but which may be the 'last straw' following a series of incidents. There is often fear of retribution if they do make a complaint. Colleagues may be reluctant to come forward as witnesses, as they too may fear the consequences for themselves. They may be so relieved not to be the subject of the bully themselves that they collude with the bully as a way of avoiding attention (see the case studies in Chapter 10).

The following terms may not quite describe what is going on in your workplace. If not, it may be useful to talk over and agree alternative phrases with your employer and other colleagues, so that everyone understands exactly what is meant by which actions. Bullying actions could take the following forms:

■ verbal abuse or a threatening attitude from a customer, colleague or manager
■ threat of assault, particularly with a weapon
■ actual assault, which can result in physical injury or sexual assault.

There is clearly some debate about the various forms of workplace bullying. An examination of the literature reveals a number of different terms used to describe the various actions that could be experienced in the workplace. For example:

■ aggression using terror tactics, open aggression, threats, shouted abuse and obscenities, or sexual or ethnic harassment
■ bullying, sometimes referred to as mobbing and harassment, which is not necessarily face-to-face but may be by written communication, e-mail (e.g. so-called 'flame-mail'), phone or automatic supervision methods (such as computer recording of downtime from work, or recording of telephone conversations, if these are not universally applied to all workers)
■ deliberately undermining a competent worker by overloading and constant criticism and humiliation about minor things, often in front of others
■ preventing individuals progressing by intentionally blocking promotion or training opportunities
■ employee abuse
■ emotional abuse
■ harassment – continual on a daily basis
■ hostile behaviours – spreading malicious rumours, or insulting someone verbally (particularly on the grounds of age, race, sex, disability, sexual orientation or religion/belief)
■ incivility, exclusion or victimization
■ job insecurity – making threats or comments without foundation
■ mistreatment/unfair treatment
■ overbearing supervision or other misuse of power or position
■ unacceptable behaviours such as copying memos/e-mails that are critical about someone to others who do not need to know, or ridiculing or demeaning someone or setting them up to fail

- unwelcome sexual advances – touching, standing too close or displaying offensive materials
- offensive, intimidating, malicious or insulting behaviour; an abuse or misuse of power through means intended to undermine, humiliate, denigrate or injure the recipient
- interpersonal conflicts between staff or between managers/supervisors and staff
- excessive supervision, monitoring everything that is done
- exclusion, victimization or unfair treatment
- withholding information so that a person cannot do their job effectively
- removing areas of responsibility from a person or constantly overruling a person's authority
- constant blocking of reasonable requests for re-scheduling a person's timetable, leave, training or promotion.

There is also the constant pressure from users, which adds to the agony. I know of one information service where one of the most senior directors caused panic among the most experienced staff whenever he appeared in the information centre because of his overbearing attitude and intolerance if some item could not be produced immediately. The head of information services had a quiet word with this user, who was horrified at what he learnt about his own behaviour. So add the following to the list of problems:

- customers – both internal and external – making unreasonable requests and then creating a scene in front of work colleagues and other customers
- intruders or customers creating a disturbance in the library or information centre.

Remember, all forms of bullying or harassment may be by an individual against another individual (perhaps the perpetrator could be someone in a position of authority such as a manager or supervisor) or involve groups of people. It may be obvious or it may be insidious. Whatever form it takes, it is unwarranted and unwelcome to the individual.

Bullying and harassment make the victim feel anxious and humiliated. Feelings of anger and frustration at being unable to cope may be triggered (see the examples in Chapter 10 'You are not Alone'). Some people may try to retaliate in some way. Others may become frightened and demotivated. Stress and the loss of self-confidence and self-esteem caused by harassment or bullying can lead to job insecurity, illness, absence from work and even resignation. Almost always, job performance is affected and relations in the workplace suffer.

Whose concern is it?

Both employer and employee should have a deep interest in reducing all forms of aggression, bullying and violence at work. For employers, violence can lead to low morale and a poor image for the organization, making it difficult to recruit staff (see also Chapter 3 'The Business Case'). It can also mean extra costs, arising from absenteeism, higher insurance premiums and compensation payments. For you as an employee, violence can cause pain, suffering and even disability or death. Physical attacks are obviously dangerous, but serious or persistent verbal abuse or threats can also damage employees' health through anxiety or stress.

There are some pieces of legislation which can be used to seek improvements in the workplace, which are described below. You should note that the terms 'he' or 'him' are often used in the legislation quoted, but the law applies to males and females alike.

All employers have a legal duty under section 2(1) of the Health and Safety at Work etc. Act 1974 to ensure 'so far as is reasonably practicable, the health, safety and welfare at work of their employees'. This duty can extend to protecting employees from assaults, aggression, bullying and other stressful situations. Every employer also has a legal duty to make a sufficient and suitable assessment of the risks to health and safety of their employees to which they are exposed while at work, so that appropriate preventative and protective measures can be introduced.

You should also be aware that under section S2(6) of the UK Health and Safety at Work etc. Act 1974, and under Regulation 4A of the Safety Representatives and Safety Committees Regulations 1977, employers have a duty to consult trade union safety representatives about health and safety matters (readers in other countries will need to find out what their health and safety legislation prescribes). See Chapter 4 for more details on management responsibilities.

Providing evidence that incidents have occurred can cause anguish for the person on the receiving end of them, because often a more senior member of staff may be responsible for the acts of aggression, bullying or discrimination.

Guidance and advice is abundant, and employers, in collaboration with their employees, will need to carry out a risk assessment (see Chapters 4 and 5 for details) and develop, within the information centre or library, a safety policy and proposed actions to tackle any form of aggression, bullying, conflict and violence at work. Such a policy and the means to carry it out will need the support and cooperation of all staff, so consultation with management, supervisors, security, personnel/human resource staff, the safety officer and staff and union safety representatives is essential. Therefore, employers must heed the requirements of the legislation and secure a safe, healthy and stress-free working environment for all those working in information centres and libraries. And employees must cooperate.

Being constantly alert

You need to remain aware that there is a possibility that any person you meet on a daily basis in your library or information centre could become agitated and reveal tensions or negative feelings hitherto unrevealed. This may have repercussions, and the chances of verbal and perhaps physical abuse may increase.

An outburst may or may not be the direct result of interaction with yourself; it could perhaps stem from a request being made which cannot be immediately fulfilled. This may add to some in-built frustration already being experienced by the individual making the request, and as a result you may experience a violent or abusive situation (see Chapter 10 for examples).

So it is necessary to learn how to react, and you should be aware that a downright unsympathetic attitude might result in increased frustration and anger, which could degenerate into a violent situation.

You should also be aware that there may be incidents where a person's behaviour may be impossible to analyse, but you do need to be trained in how to alleviate such situations or indeed prevent them from getting worse (see some of the incidents cited in Chapter 10 'You are not Alone').

Training is essential. It will help you to identify the possible causes of such incidents, and provide you with information and skills on how to avoid them. If they do occur you will be better equipped to deal with potentially violent situations. There is more information on training in Chapter 8.

How this behaviour can affect you

Both immediate and long-term effects may result from aggression, bullying and violence. You should be aware of the following repercussions.

Psychological effects

Victims of violent behaviour lose self-confidence and self-esteem, and are at risk of suffering from stress. This, if not adequately treated, may develop into problems of anxiety or depression.

Physical effects

An injury may need treatment, including surgery. Serious injuries have led to long-term disability, and the possibility of not being able to carry on with a career.

Stress and its effects

Continuous pressures or other excessive demands place a great deal of stress on individuals. Stress is associated with a wide range of ill-health problems and can affect you in a number of ways:

■ stress-related physical effects: headaches/migraine, dizziness, raised heartbeat, sweating, blurred vision, loss of appetite, inability to sleep, skin diseases, sickness, irritable bowels, aching neck and shoulders and lowering of resistance to infection

■ stress-related psychological and behavioural effects: anxiety, irritability, depression, poor concentration, tendency to consume more alcohol and tobacco, tearfulness and inability to deal with everyday tasks and situations in a calm/controlled manner.

You should be aware that the effects of stress are usually short-lived, and cause no lasting harm if the pressures are short-lived. However, you should be warned that where pressures are intense and continuous for some time, the effects of stress can be far more sustained, leading eventually to longer-term psychological problems and physical ill-health.

The UK's Health and Safety Executive warns that stress is associated with a number of serious ill-health conditions such as high blood pressure, thyroid disorders, ulcers, heart disease, anxiety and depression.

All this can have a secondary effect on the success of the library or information centre's services: it can create a bad atmosphere, which affects customers, and could, if you are in a 'business-oriented service', lead to a loss of business, with the attendant loss of sales and profit to consider. If staff loss through resignation is involved, then this in turn could add to staff costs due to the need to recruit and retrain valuable staff. Loss of staff can in itself put extra pressure on the staff that remain, and could cause some further aggression. Repeated failure to respond to staff complaints could possibly result in a constructive dismissal claim, which may result in public exposure through cases being taken to industrial tribunals and being reported in the media.

You, as an employee, should be aware that employers need to be able to provide evidence that they are taking steps to look after their staff, but first of all it will be necessary to decide whether there is a problem.

Making sure you are safe

Considering risks should be part of your everyday thinking. You should appreciate that risks at work do not exist just at your desk or counter, or just in your library or information centre. There may be risks in travelling to and from work or in connection with your work; in work that you might do on someone else's premises; or in car parks, lifts, corridors, etc. You should be aware that time spent away from home or travelling abroad might involve work-related risks.

Legislation requires employers to secure the personal safety of their employees, but you should remember that personal safety is a shared responsibility between employer and employee, so you also have a responsibility to help yourself to be safe.

You should also think about the personal safety of others: family, colleagues, work contacts and friends. You should acquire skills and strategies that become almost instinctive, so that if a difficult – and potentially violent – situation arises, you have the confidence to know what to do (see the section on training in Chapter 8).

Deciding if there is a problem

Your employer may think that aggression, bullying, conflict and violence is not a problem at your workplace, or that incidents are rare. However, you as an employee may have a different view.

The easiest way to find out is to ask your colleagues. This can be done informally through contact with managers, supervisors, safety representatives or trade union representatives. Alternatively, your manager may agree to circulate a questionnaire. The idea is to find out whether you or any colleagues ever feel threatened or under great stress. The results of such a survey should be published so that if there is a problem, everyone will realize that the manager recognizes it, and if there is not, any fears will be allayed.

Even if no problem is found, it is wise to check the position again from time to time, because things can change. See also Chapters 4 and 5.

The first steps

The first steps which should be taken by management in making an assessment of whether there are any forms of aggression, bullying, conflict and violence in the workplace are:

■ consult with colleagues
■ build up a picture of incidents

- set up a formal procedure to report any incidents
- classify all incidents
- keep records of incidents where staff are injured (this is a legal duty under various pieces of legislation: the Management of Health and Safety at Work Regulations 1999 (amended in 2006), the Reporting of Injuries, Diseases and Dangerous Occurrences Regulations 1995 and the Protection from Harassment Act 1997)
- ensure that reports are made
- search for suitable preventative measures
- decide what to do
- put the measures into practice.

Record all incidents

It is the duty of your manager to keep a detailed record of all incidents, so a picture can be built up if there is a problem. A simple report form (as suggested by the Health and Safety Executive and other organizations) can be used to record the details of what happened: where, when, who was involved and any possible causes (see Chapters 3, 4, 5 and 6 for more details and sample forms).

You should be aware that your colleagues may not report incidents for all sorts of reasons. Perhaps they accept aggressive behaviour as part of the job. They may think it will reflect badly on them if they admit it happens. They may be worried about their job security. Be aware that some employers are reluctant to admit that any form of aggression is taking place in their organization.

Sometimes, victims of aggression are unable to recognize the unfair treatment they are receiving.

There can be many reasons why incidents are not reported:

- Where an aggressive management style is in place, staff can be afraid to complain in case they are seen to be against management.
- There may be a misunderstanding of the difference between assertiveness and aggression.

■ Some individual incidents may appear trivial, but it is the repetitiveness of these incidents which is important.

■ Men may not want to complain because it may appear unmasculine.

■ Staff may be reluctant to complain because there are no witnesses.

■ Victims may feel that any complaint may result in further action by the aggressor (the playground effect).

■ Victims may be afraid to complain because they think management may regard it as their inability to cope.

Therefore, all staff, whatever their level/grade, should be encouraged to report all incidents. Having a report form available will help you and your colleagues to realize that this is what is expected.

Classify all incidents

You, your colleagues and manager will want to know what kinds of incidents are happening. This means classifying them under various headings: place, time, type of incident, who was involved and possible causes.

For example, Table 2.1 gives a simple classification to help you decide how serious incidents are.

Table 2.1 Classification of incidents

Type of incident	Result
Involving physical contact	Fatal injury Minor injury Injury or emotional shock requiring first aid, out-patient treatment, counselling and/or absence from work (record number of days)
Involving serious or persistent threats of verbal abuse	Emotional shock requiring counselling and/or absence from work (record number of days) Feeling of being at risk or under great stress

It should be easy to classify 'minor injuries' but the manager will have to decide how to classify 'serious or persistent verbal abuse' for your organization, so as to cover all incidents that worry staff.

The manager can use the details on the incident report forms, along with the classifications, to check for patterns: common causes, work areas, or times of day or night. Remedies can then be targeted where they are needed most. For example, a survey by a trade union after 12 separate shop robberies found that each incident occurred between five and seven o'clock in the evening.

This type of finding may be useful for your management when deciding whether security is needed for late night opening of information centres and libraries.

POINTS TO REFLECT ON . . .

■ Do you understand the various forms of aggression, bullying, conflict, harassment and violence that can occur in information centres and libraries?

■ Does your employer have a health and safety policy?

■ Does your employer have a harassment policy?

■ Are you now aware of the range of legislation that protects you at work?

3 The business case

This chapter shows that tackling the problems of aggression, bullying, conflict, harassment and violence at work brings business benefits. It covers the following:

■ managing change positively by keeping staff involved and informed
■ dealing with organizational pressures: internal conflict, managerial pressure and external pressures (e.g. outsourcing, downsizing)
■ the case for management making a firm anti-bullying commitment to staff
■ the deleterious effect of aggression, bullying and stress on staff turnover and costs, attendance levels, recruitment and retention, customer satisfaction, and organizational image and reputation
■ potential litigation.

Management of change – keeping staff involved and informed

Change is, or should be, happening all the time in workplaces, especially in libraries and the information sector because of the nature of the work involved – there is a constant flow of new technologies, new information sources, new ways of doing jobs, new supervisors and managers, new colleagues, new demands from customers and new customers, for example if you are working in higher education or in public libraries. Whatever sector you are working in, you will experience this constant flow of changes. Some people thrive on change, others initiate change, while some just hate change of any sort. Sometimes changes cause conflict and it is here that management at all levels must be on their mettle – to anticipate, debate and be prepared to manage any possible internal conflict.

Keeping staff involved in change of any sort is one sure way of moving changes along without conflict. Staff, especially in libraries, have been employed for their knowledge and experience. The alert manager will gain much by asking questions and discussing changes and potential changes with staff at all levels. After all, those doing the actual job will have a good idea of what will suceed and what will cause problems.

Dealing with internal conflict, managerial pressure and external pressures

Dealing with internal conflict, managerial pressure and external pressures, such as outsourcing and downsizing, can be stressful in itself for all levels of staff. For many years, workplace conflict has been viewed as dysfunctional, destructive and damaging – a generally undesirable by-product of working life. Nevertheless, given the rising diversity within the labour market, increasingly complex and ever-changing work environments, shifting attitudes to management and changing expectations of employees and employers, workplace conflict is now an inevitable and inescapable reality for every organization regardless of size, shape or structure. Many things can cause it, and all employers and employees will need to know that internal conflict arises for many reasons:

- lack of control over work
- excessive time pressures
- excessive or inflexible working hours
- too much or too little work or responsibility
- confusion about duties and responsibilities
- lack of job variety and interest
- inadequate training and possibilities for learning new skills
- poor work/life balance
- difficult relationships at work
- lack of support and lack of contact with colleagues

■ organizational confusion, restructuring and/or job changes
■ uncertainty over job prospects.

Conflict management refers to the variety of ways in which people handle grievances – clashes of right and wrong. In the information world it includes such diverse phenomena as gossip, ridicule, feuding and downright provocation by colleagues, managers and customers. Which of the diverse forms of conflict management will be used in any given case is predicted and explained by the social structure – or social geometry – of the case.

But what is absolutely clear is that the management must 'grasp the nettle' and deal immediately with any form of conflict.

Management commitment to staff

It is essential that management should give strong signals at all times that no form of aggression will be tolerated in the workplace. This commitment should be stated right from the beginning – in job adverts, at the job interview, in the induction course and when a person starts the job.

Successful businesses are built on good internal and external relationships. Yet even in the best-run organizations, conflict is inevitable. People come to work with diverse beliefs, histories, needs and aspirations, and these do not always fit neatly into the organization's context. Management will need to focus on the skills required to build good relationships, to minimize the risk of conflict and to deal with it in a constructive manner. This strong commitment should be reinforced in conflict, harassment, health and safety policy statements, and encouragement to staff to attend training courses.

Strong management or bullying?

Andrea Adams, the well-known campaigner, says:

> Bullying is a sustained form of psychological abuse and often emanates from a senior person taking what they feel is a 'strong line' with employees. There is, however, a fine line between strong management and bullying. That line is crossed when the target of bullying is persistently downgraded with the result

that they begin to show signs of being distressed, becoming either physically, mentally or psychologically hurt. It can be distinguished from other work related problems, in that it is not the intention of the perpetrator, but the deed itself and its impact on the recipient or target that constitutes workplace bullying.

(www.andreaadams.trust.org, see Appendix C)

It can be seen in the literature and also in the guidance and advice from experts that bullying in all formats thrives where it is common behaviour across the management hierarchy. This is seen especially in highly competitive environments, where many individuals consider bullying to be the accepted method of motivating staff. In organizations that pride themselves on strong management, bullying can soon become part of the business's culture, and management will be seen by their employees to have condoned such behaviour simply through inaction.

As discussed in Chapter 2, some employees may feel that they have to put up with bullying behaviour as part of the job, and may not wish to complain for fear of losing their job, further victimization or being labelled a troublemaker. However, what sort of workplace can really condone a form of behaviour which engenders fear in employees? People cannot contribute their best when in fear of harassment, bullying or abuse.

Staffing issues affected by aggression in the workplace
Employee commitment to work – staff performance and productivity

Most employees want to do a good day's work. Some may need more motivating than others, but in general where there is a culture of personal as well as organizational achievement staff want to give of their best. They want to contribute to the quality of the work being carried out, and bask in the knowledge that they are appreciated, not only by their line management but also by their customers.

If there is strong management commitment to ensuring that the workplace is free from such problems, then the library will be successful, staff will be able to get on with their work and customers will be happy.

Staff turnover, intention to leave and costs

Staff performance and productivity will always be affected if there are underlying problems of aggression etc. in the workplace. This will be manifest in staff turnover or the knowledge that staff will leave when opportunity arises.

The CIPD's *People Management* (CIPD, 2006b) notes that 25% of people who have been bullied and 20% of witnesses leave the organization. To understand the cost involved, management will first need to calculate the average employee replacement cost, including human resources/personnel time and management time before, during and after the interview, plus training costs and time before the new recruit becomes fully effective. The CIPD also suggests that management will need to consider the incidence of bullying and estimate a 'normal figure' of 10% if no data exist. Then, multiply the total number of people working in the library by the estimated incidence of bullying and by 0.25 (the typical proportion of people who have to leave) to get to the number of employees who will have to be replaced, and multiply by the average employee replacement cost. Add to this witness replacement costs, based on a conservative estimate of two witnesses per situation.

Other direct costs include early retirement and severance payments in other cases that can be tracked back to bullying. Legal and investigation costs should also be added in to reach the final cost.

Attendance levels

Research shows that where line managers have training in absence management, there is a decrease in sickness absence rates. However, many libraries provide very little or no training to line managers, and therefore fail to reap the benefits of effective absence management. In later chapters and in Appendices A and B, you will find tools that have been developed to help managers with absence management. Managers need to be able to:

- identify an absence problem
- develop an absence strategy

■ deal with short-term absence
■ deal with long-term absence.

Staff recruitment and retention

Good staff recruitment and retention is vital if the library wants to suceed. For example, hearing about incidents may make the job less attractive to potential recruits, and experienced staff may leave a job if they no longer feel safe or able to cope. Sick leave can result from stress-related health problems or a physical injury following a violent incident.

High levels of sick leave, staff refusal to do certain jobs, high insurance premiums and compensation claims, and a breakdown in the relationship with clients can all have a detrimental impact on a library's productivity and profitability.

Other issues affected by aggression in the workplace
Customer satisfaction

The customer is king, or so the saying goes, and this is true for libraries and information services, whichever sector they are in. Nothing is more satisfying for staff and management than to have an appreciative customer base. Without customers, what is the point? With the aid of technology, libraries can reach outside their walls and offer a wider variety of services than ever before, but will only do so if there is a movitated staff and management working together to ensure that the working environment is free from stress, conflict, bullying and aggression.

Organizational image and reputation

City employee subjected to workplace bullying: £800,000 compensation

This type of newspaper headline does nothing for the image of any organization, let alone an organization such as the Deutsche Bank. This example reports that an ex-employee of Deutsche Bank in London was awarded £800,000 compensation in the High Court following a successful claim under the Protection from Harrassment Act 1997. The claimant was subjected to a sustained campaign of bullying and had two nervous breakdowns, but management failed to intervene to stop the bullying.

Litigation

There are many other such situations where cases have been upheld in court and substantial awards been made to victims. Employers' legal requirement to protect employees from stress was underlined in a landmark court case in 1996, when Northumberland County Council was ordered to pay £175,000 in compensation to a former employee, social worker John Walker, who had suffered two nervous breakdowns as a result of stress at work.

Since then there have been other high profile cases, but proving a stress case against an employer is still not easy. In the case of John Walker, the case against his employer was watertight. He complained to his management that he was having problems with his workload and that he was under stress. They said, 'Fine, fine'. He had a nervous breakdown. Management negotiated his return to work, promising to make the conditions better. Nothing happened. He came back to work and had a second breakdown. It was the second breakdown that won the case.

To win compensation in court, a victim of workplace stress must do more than prove that they have been injured by stress. They must also establish:

- that the duty of care was breached by the employer
- that the employer's negligence caused the stress (stress caused by factors outside work, such as marital problems, does not count)
- that they had already raised the problem with their employer
- that the stress was reasonably foreseeable.

Is it my concern?

As can be seen, from the above, both employer and employee have an interest in reducing all forms of harassment, aggression, bullying, conflict and violence at work. For employers, this kind of behaviour can lead to poor morale and a poor image for the organization, creating difficulties in recruiting and keeping staff. It can also involve extra costs, through absenteeism, higher insurance premiums and compensation payments.

For employees, such forms of behaviour can cause pain, distress and even disability or death. Physical attacks are obviously very dangerous, but serious or persistent verbal abuse or threats can also damage employees' health through anxiety or stress.

Protecting against litigation

Some progress has been made over the last ten years or so, with new advice and guidance to protect against litigation, but you can never entirely eliminate accidents, fatalities and all other workplace incidents and problems. However, management can guard against them by implementing a robust health and safety management system that can guard against litigation, protect against copycat cases and, in the most extreme case, protect staff from a potential prison sentence.

If there is a robust health and safety system all employees will know where they can go for help and advice, unless there is a weak and wimpish management that prefers to sweep things under the carpet. We will see that this does actually happen in Chapter 10.

POINTS TO REFLECT ON . . .

■ Do you understand that managing change means keeping staff involved and informed?

■ Are you aware that there are many reasons for internal conflict?

■ Do you appreciate that employees need to make a commitment to work – as do managerial staff?

■ Do you recognize why the organization's image and reputation can be damaged by internal conflict and harassment?

4 Risk assessment

Whether you are an individual employee or part of a management team, this chapter will give you information on:

■ the need for risk assessments
■ the legal responsibilities of employers as regards risk assessment
■ what a risk assessment actually is
■ the five steps involved in risk assessment.

The need for risk assessments

Workplace problems caused by employees, managers and others are rarely discussed before events force them into the open and the organization is faced with possible disciplinary procedures, accusations of unfair dismissal and even industrial tribunals.

Listing aggression, violence and bullying as hazards alongside physical aspects of the workplace such as heat, light, ventilation, dangerous equipment and practice provides an opportunity for rational and purposeful discussion and the development of agreed procedures for dealing with what are often regarded as taboo subjects.

In larger organizations it is probable that a risk assessment has been carried out covering premises and equipment, but this can be extended within a section or department such as the library and information service to include aggression, bullying, conflict, harassment, stress and violence either in response to a known problem or to provide a basis for the development of formal arrangements to deal with possible future situations.

Legal responsibilities

You should be aware that it is the duty of every employer under the Management of Health and Safety at Work Regulations 1999 (see Appendix D) to make a suitable and sufficient assessment of:

a) the risks to the health and safety of his employees to which they are exposed whilst they are at work; and

b) the risks to health and safety of persons not in his employment arising out of or in connection with the conduct by him of his undertaking, for the purpose of identifying the measures he needs to take to comply with the requirements and prohibitions imposed upon him by or under the relevant statutory provisions.

The regulations also state:

If you are a *self-employed person* you will need to make a suitable and sufficient assessment of:

a) the risks to your own health and safety to which you are exposed whilst you are at a place of work; and

b) the risks to health and safety of persons not in your employment arising out of or in connection with the conduct by you or your undertaking, for the purpose of identifying the measures you need to take to comply with the requirements and prohibitions imposed upon you by or under the relevant statutory provisions.

Any assessment such as is referred to in the paragraphs above needs to be reviewed, as stated in the same regulations above, by your employer or a self-employed person who made the assessment if:

a) there is reason to suspect that it is no longer valid; or

b) there has been a significant change in the matters to which it relates; and where as a result of any such review changes to an assessment are required, the employer or self-employed person concerned shall make them.

Where the employer employs five or more employees, he shall record:

a) the significant findings of the assessment; and
b) any group of his employees identified by it as being especially at risk.

What is a risk assessment?

A risk assessment is simply a careful examination of what, in your work-place, could cause harm to people, so that you can weigh up whether enough precautions have been taken or whether more should be done to prevent harm. Workers and others have a right to be protected from harm caused by a failure to take reasonable control measures.

Accidents and ill health can ruin lives and affect any business, including libraries – if output is lost, insurance costs increase or you have to go to court. The owners of a library are legally required to assess the risks in the workplace and put in place a plan to control those risks, just as any other business.

The UK's Health and Safety Executive (HSE) believes that risk management should be about practical steps to protect people from real harm and suffering – not just bureaucratic back covering. If you believe some of the stories you hear, health and safety is all about stopping any activity that might possibly lead to harm. This is not the HSE's vision of sensible health and safety – they want to save lives, not stop them. The approach is to seek a balance between the unachievable aim of absolute safety and the kind of poor management of risk that damages lives and the economy.

The HSE has worked with a very wide range of organizations to identify some principles of sensible risk management that set out what risk management should and should not be about. The HSE is intent on ensuring sensible risk management, and has launched revised guidance on risk assessment to make clearer what is and what is not expected.

Sensible risk management *is* about:

■ ensuring that employees and the public are properly protected
■ providing overall benefit to society by balancing benefits and risks, with a focus on reducing real risks – both those which are relatively

common and those which are less common but have serious consequences

■ enabling innovation and learning, not stifling them
■ ensuring that those who create risks manage them responsibly and understand that failure to manage real risks responsibly is likely to lead to legal action
■ enabling individuals to understand that as well as the right to protection, they also have an obligation to exercise responsibility.

Sensible risk management is *not* about:

■ creating a totally risk-free society
■ generating useless paperwork mountains
■ scaring people by exaggerating or publicizing trivial risks
■ stopping important recreational and learning activities for individuals where the risks are managed
■ reducing protection of people from risks that cause real harm and suffering.

Ideally, every organization should have in their health and safety policy a stress and harassment section so that all staff, at all levels, are clear about what is acceptable behaviour and what is not. There could be a standalone stress and harassment policy structured in the same way as the health and safety policy.

A risk assessment is an important step towards protecting workers and businesses, as well as complying with the law. It helps you focus on the risks that really matter in your workplace – the ones with the potential to cause real harm. In many instances, straightforward basic measures can readily control risks, for example ensuring that spillages are cleaned up promptly so people do not slip, or that cupboard drawers are kept closed to ensure people do not trip. In most situations, this involves simple, cheap and effective measures to ensure that the most valuable asset – the workforce – is protected.

The law does not expect anyone to eliminate all risk, but there is a requirement to protect people as far as is 'reasonably practicable'.

Five steps to risk assessment

Follow these five steps to assess the risks in your workplace:

1 Identify the hazards.
2 Decide who might be harmed and how.
3 Evaluate the risks and decide on the necessary precautions.
4 Record your findings and implement them.
5 Review your assessment and update if necessary.

These are explained in more detail below, and in the next chapter.

A manager should not overcomplicate the process. In many organizations, the risks are well known and the necessary control measures are easy to apply. You probably already know whether, for example, you have employees who move heavy loads and so could harm their backs, or where people are most likely to slip or trip. If so, check that you have taken reasonable precautions to avoid injury.

If you run a small organization and you are confident you understand what is involved, you can do the assessment yourself. You do not have to be a health and safety expert.

If you work in a large organization, you could ask the health and safety adviser or human resource manager to help you. In all cases, you should make sure that you involve your staff and their representatives in the process. This is particularly relevant when considering possible risks arising from aggression and violence.They will have useful information about how the work is done that will make your assessment of the risk more thorough and effective. But remember: managers are responsible for seeing that the assessment is carried out properly.

When thinking about your risk assessment, remember that a hazard is anything that may cause harm, such as chemicals, electricity, working from ladders and steps, an open drawer, manual handling, etc. To this list you should add potential aggression and violence from colleagues and users of the service, both internal and external.

The risk is the chance, high or low, that somebody could be harmed by these and other hazards, together with an indication of how serious the harm could be – for example, in extreme cases, a nervous breakdown. Risk therefore reflects both the likelihood that harm will occur and its severity.

In some cases, this detailed approach may not be necessary; all the hazards may be known and the risks readily apparent, and can therefore be addressed directly.

This is not the only way to do a risk assessment. There are other methods that work well, particularly for more complex risks and circumstances. However, this method is the most straightforward for most organizations.

POINTS TO REFLECT ON . . .

- Do you understand what a risk assessment is and why it is needed?
- Has your management done a risk assessment?
- Does your employer have a health and safety policy?
- Does your employer have a harassment policy?
- Are you now aware of the legislation that exists to protect you at work?
- Do you feel that enough has been done to ensure that yours is a safe and healthy workplace?

5 Carrying out risk assessments

Whether you are an individual employee or part of a management team, this chapter will give you information on:

■ how a risk assessment should be carried out
■ what happens at each step
■ some Frequently Asked Questions.

How a risk assessment should be carried out

As discussed in Chapter 4, the purpose of a risk assessment is to help the employer or self-employed person determine what measures should be taken to comply with their duties under the 'relevant statutory provisions'. This phrase covers the general duties in the Health and Safety at Work etc. Act 1974 (HASAWA) and the more specific duties in the various Acts and Regulations associated with the HASAWA.

Regulation 3 of the Management of Health and Safety at Work Regulations does not itself stipulate the measures to be taken as a result of risk assessment. The measures taken in each workplace will derive from compliance with other health and safety duties as described above, taking carefully into account the risk assessment. In essence, the risk assessment guides the judgement of the employer or the self-employed person as regards the measures they ought to take to fulfil their statutory obligations.

What happens at each step

Being able to make a judgement about the hazards in your daily life is useful, and the following advice may help when assessing the workplace. An initial risk assessment should always include any known information (e.g. data collected).

Step 1: Identify the hazards

If you are doing the assessment yourself, walk around your workplace and look afresh at what could reasonably be expected to cause harm. Ignore the trivial and concentrate only on significant hazards which could result in serious harm or affect several people.

Ask your fellow employees or their representatives what they think. They may have noticed things that are not immediately obvious, including irrational behaviour, a 'poor atmosphere', lack of co-operation, unwelcome visitors and occurrences of bullying.

A risk assessment for aggression etc. aims to identify the causes of stressors or potential stressors that may be harmful to the health and well-being of staff members. Remember that some stressors, once identified, can be removed.

The HR department may have reports of what is causing ill-health within the organization which could be used to identify any trends. Also, look at exit interview reports to see whether they contain any information of use in identifying hazards.

Step 2: Decide who might be harmed, and how

In addition to regular employees, think about people who may not be in the workplace all the time: cleaners, visitors, contractors, maintenance personnel, etc. Include members of the public, or people you share your workplace with, if there is a chance they could be hurt by being in or near your activities.

Step 3: Evaluate the risks arising from the hazards and decide whether existing precautions are adequate

Even after all precautions have been taken, some risk usually remains. What you have to decide for each significant hazard is whether this remaining risk is high, medium or low. First, ask yourself whether your employers have done all the things that the law says they have got to do. Then ask yourself whether generally accepted industry standards are in place. But don't stop there – think for yourself, because the law also says that you must do what is reasonably practicable to keep your workplace safe. Your real aim is to make all risks small by adding to your precautions if necessary. More information about legal requirements and standards can be found in the HSE publications *Management of Health and Safety at Work Regulations: approved code of practice* (see Appendix D), the very useful *Essentials of Health and Safety at Work* (2006) and the *Management Standards for Tackling Work-related Stress* (2004) (see Appendix A). You can also check the HSE website www.hse.gov.uk.

If you find that something needs to be done, ask yourself:

■ Can you and your manager get rid of the hazard altogether?
■ If not, how can you and your manager control the risks so that harm is unlikely?

If the work you do tends to vary a lot, or if you or your colleagues move from one site to another (e.g. working in branch libraries or mobile libraries), select those hazards which you can reasonably foresee and assess the risks from them. After that, if you spot any unusual hazard when you get to a site, get information from others on-site and take what action is agreed to be necessary.

If your employer shares a workplace, your employer must tell the other employers and self-employed people there about any risks that the work could cause them, and what precautions are being taken. Also, your manager must think about the risks to you and your colleagues from those who share your workplace.

Step 4: Record the findings and implement them

If your employer has fewer than five employees, he does not need to write anything down, but if there are five or more employees the employer must record the significant findings of the assessment. This means writing down the more significant hazards and recording the most important conclusions. The employees must be informed about the findings.

There is no need for your employer to show how he did the assessment, provided he can show:

■ that a proper check was made
■ who might be affected
■ that he dealt with all the obvious significant hazards, taking into account the number of people who could be involved
■ that the precautions are reasonable, and the remaining risk is low
■ that the results were communicated to all staff.

Assessments need to be suitable and sufficient, and the following important questions need to be asked:

■ Are the precautions reasonable?
■ Is there something to show that a proper check was made?

Your employer should keep the written document for future reference or use; it can help if a health and safety inspector questions the precautions, or if anyone becomes involved in any action for civil liability. It can also remind you to keep an eye on particular matters. And it helps to show that the employer has done what the law requires.

Figure 5.1 shows a sample risk assessment form which you and your employers may find helpful, but you may wish to produce your own version tailormade to your specific needs.

To make things simpler, you can refer to other documents, such as manuals, the health and safety policy statement, company rules, manufacturers' instructions and health and safety procedures. These may already list hazards and precautions. Your employer does not need to repeat all of these in written documents, and it is up to your employer whether all the

Named hazard (include date of inspection)	What is the risk of injury to employees?	Steps taken (or to take) to avoid injury (include date)

Figure 5.1 Sample risk assessment form

instructions on hazards and precautions are combined together in one document, or kept separately.

Step 5: Review risk assessment from time to time and revise if necessary

Sooner or later, a new layout of the working environment, new equipment, substances and/or procedures will be introduced which could lead to new problems or hazards. The assessment should be amended to take account of the new problem/hazard.

In any case it is good practice to review assessments from time to time. Do not make trivial changes, but if there are significant new hazards, these need to be considered in their own right and action taken to keep the risks down.

Also, ensure that there are opportunities to report any unsatisfactory working conditions and steps taken to rectify them. You should also look at Chapters 6 and 7 for details of where improvements in the working environment could be made.

Make sure that your employer plans and organizes work for all employees so as to prevent as reasonably as possible any opportunities for victimization. Your employer will need to implement countermeasures without delay if signs of aggression become apparent in any part of the workplace. This should include an investigation of whether the work procedures are the cause.

No one expects a risk assessment to be perfect, but it must be suitable and sufficient. Management will need to be able to show that the following actions were carried out:

■ Premises and equipment were checked.
■ Staff were asked who might be affected.
■ All the obvious significant hazards were checked, taking into account the number of people who could be involved.
■ The precautions are reasonable, and the remaining risk is low.
■ Staff or their representatives were involved in the process.

The HSE has a risk assessment template available for organizations to use: see www.hse.gov.uk/risk/template.pdf.

If, like many organizations, you find that there are quite a lot of improvements that you could make, big and small, don't try to do everything at once. Make a plan of action to deal with the most important things first. Health and safety inspectors acknowledge the efforts of businesses that are clearly trying to make improvements.

A good plan of action often includes a mixture of different things, such as:

■ a few cheap and/or easy improvements that can be done quickly, perhaps as a temporary solution until more reliable controls are in place
■ long-term solutions, including training about those risks most likely to cause accidents or ill-health
■ long-term solutions to those risks with the worst potential consequences
■ arrangements for training employees about the main risks that remain, and how they are to be controlled
■ regular checks to make sure that the control measures stay in place
■ clear lines of responsibility, including who will lead on what action, and by when.

Remember, prioritize and tackle the most important things first. As you complete each action, tick it off your plan.

Most of all, the employer should provide rapid help and support to any victim (see Chapter 9 for further information).

Few workplaces stay the same, but when you are busy running a business such as a library it's all too easy to forget about reviewing your risk assessment – until something has gone wrong and it is too late. Why not set up a rolling programme with a review date for this risk assessment now? Note it in your diary as an annual event.

During the year, if there is a significant change, do not wait: check your risk assessment and, where necessary, amend it. If possible, it is best to think about the risk assessment when you're planning your change – that way, you leave yourself more flexibility.

Some Frequently Asked Questions

What if the work carried out tends to vary a lot, or employees move from one site to another, such as employees working in branch libraries or in a mobile library?

Identify the hazards you can reasonably expect and assess the risks from them. This general assessment should stand you in good stead for the majority of your work. Where you do take on work or a new site that is different, cover any new or different hazards with a specific assessment. You do not have to start from scratch each time.

What if the workplace is shared with others?

Tell the other employers and self-employed people there about any risks your work could cause them, and what precautions you are taking. Also, think about the risks to your own workforce from those who share your workplace.

Do employees have responsibilities?

Yes. Employees have a legal responsibility to co-operate with their employer's efforts to improve health and safety. For example, they must know who is responsible and can take action when necessary, and employees must look out for each other. Any health and safety policy, including any stress and harassment policy, must be adhered to by all employees.

What if an employee's circumstances change?

The risk assessment must be looked at again. You are required to carry out a specific risk assessment for new or expectant mothers, as some tasks (heavy lifting) may not be appropriate. If an employee develops a disability then you are required to make reasonable adjustments. People returning to work following major surgery may also have particular requirements. If you put your mind to it, you can almost always find a way forward that works for you and your employees.

What if some risks have already been assessed?

If, for example, you use hazardous chemicals and you have already assessed the risks to health and the precautions you need to take under the Control of Substances Hazardous to Health Regulations (COSHH), you can consider them 'checked' and move on.

What are the various formats of aggression, bullying, conflict, harassment and violence at work? How will I recognize what is what?

Look at Chapter 2 for causes and how to recognize what is what and why it happens in libraries. Also look at Chapter 3 'The Business Case'.

What should my employer be doing?

Look at Chapter 2, which gives details of what employers should be doing and how employees should be on constant alert. Also look at Chapter 3 'The Business Case' followed by Chapters 4 and 5.

What is risk assessment? Does it really apply to libraries?

Chapter 4 describes what exactly risk assessment is, who should be involved and how it can be done – and yes, it applies to all workplaces with more than five employees.

Is there any legislation that I can use if I am suffering from stress and conflict?

Chapter 4 outlines the need for risk assessment and also informs you about the legal responsibilities of employers and the pieces of legislation that must be implemented. See also Appendix D for a list of relevant legislation.

I want to read more about stress and conflict. Where can I get authoritative advice and guidance?

The major sources are quoted in Chapter 6 but there is also a Bibliography in Appendix A, and a list of organizations and websites that will be able to give advice and guidance (see Appendices C and D). In addition, you can arrange a 15-day free trial of OSH UPDATE (www.oshupdate.com) to check for yourself the vast amount of authoritative and validated information and legislation.

Management does not think there is a problem – what actions can I take?

Investigate! Ask your health and safety manager/adviser, your HR manager or your safety representative to help. Ask if there are any reports on continuous absenteeism available, and ask your colleagues if they have any problems.

If you think you are at risk from work-related aggression, bullying, conflict, harassment and violence, do not give up. There is a wealth of information available to help you.

POINTS TO REFLECT ON . . .
- Do you understand the details of each step in the risk assessment?
- Do you know where to go for a risk assessment template?
- Did the Frequently Asked Questions answer your queries?
- Do you know what to do if your management team does not think there is a problem?

6 Advice, guidance and legislation galore

In this chapter you will find information on:

■ legislation and publications that will help you
■ where to go for guidance and advice (UK, European and international)
■ preventative measures
■ steps you could take if your management team does not recognize that there is a problem.

Legislation that will help you

Health and safety law applies to risks from stress and violence, just as it does to other risks from work. The main pieces of relevant legislation that will be of interest are:

1 The Health and Safety at Work etc. Act 1974: Employers have a legal duty under this Act to ensure, as far as is reasonably practicable, the health, safety and welfare at work of their employees.
2 The Management of Health and Safety at Work Regulations 1999 SI 1999 No. 3242: Employers must consider the risks to employees (including the risk of reasonably foreseeable stress and violence), decide how significant these risks are, decide what to do to prevent or control the risks and develop a clear management plan to achieve this.
3 The Reporting of Injuries, Diseases and Dangerous Occurrences Regulations 1995 (RIDDOR) SI 1995 No. 3163: Employers must notify their enforcing authority in the event of an accident at work to

any employee resulting in death, major injury or incapacity for normal work for three or more days. This includes any act of physical violence done to a person at work.

4 Safety Representatives and Safety Committees Regulations 1977 (a) and The Health and Safety (Consultation with Employees) Regulations 1996 (b) SI 1977 No. 500: Employers must inform, and consult with, employees in good time on matters relating to their health and safety. Employee representatives, either appointed by recognized trade unions under (a) or elected under (b) may make representations to their employers on matters affecting the health and safety of those they represent.

5 The Protection from Harassment Act 1997: This Act makes provision for protecting people from harassment and similar conduct. A person must not pursue a course of conduct which amounts to harassment of another, or which he/she knows or ought to know amounts to harassment of others.

6 Human Rights Act 1998: This came into force on 2 October 2000. It incorporates and brings into force the provisions of the European Convention on Human Rights.

7 The Employment Equality (Age) Regulations 2006 SI No. 2006 No. 1031: This came into force on 1 October 2006 and covers age discrimination.

8 The Employment Act 2002 (Dispute Resolution) Regulations 2004 SI 2004 No. 752: As of 1 October 2004 this has set new rules which all employers have to follow in dispute resolution.

9 The Employment Equality (Sex Discrimination) Regulations 2005 SI 2005 No. 2467: Under this piece of legislation, any form of harassment is unlawful.

10 Employment Rights Act 1996 – especially the parts dealing with unfair dismissal, constructive dismissal and victimization.

Regardless of their size, all employers have to have in place minimum statutory procedures for dealing with dismissal, disciplinary action and grievances in the workplace. There is a legal requirement for them to inform their employees of these procedures. The ACAS website is very informative (see www.acas.org.uk) and tells you what you need to know about the legislation, as well as providing guidance, training materials, etc. (e.g. the Dispute Resolution Procedures that amend the Schedules to the Employment Act 2002, concerning the duty on employers and employees to follow dispute resolution procedures: failure by either party to follow these procedures will affect the way in which an employment tribunal will consider claims). The legislation is available on the Office of Public Sector Information (OPSI) website (see www.opsi.gov.uk).

Guidance and advice

In the last ten years, there has been prolific growth in the amount of guidance and advice issued, not only by official government bodies but also by a range of organizations that do sterling work in helping people come to grips with workplace problems. A list of organizations, with contact details, brief description and website addresses, can be found in the Appendices, as can an extensive reading list.

Preventative measures
Publications that will help you

There are now countless publications on risk management, conflict resolution, aggression, bullying, stress and violence in the workplace. Some are listed in the Bibliography (see Appendix A). A search through the collection of worldwide authoritative databases in OSH UPDATE, which includes HSELINE, CISDOC and NIOSHTICS (see www.oshupdate.com), will lead to a wider range of full text documents and references for further reading that include the UK's Health and Safety Executive publications. These give further guidance and advice on combating aggression, bullying, conflict, harassment and violence in the workplace.

Have you or your manager taken all the necessary precautions that will secure a safer working environment for you and other staff? The Health and Safety Executive has produced a number of publications that will certainly help. Real Solutions, Real People (ISBN 0-7176-2767-5) is a comprehensive pack designed to help employers identify risks associated with work-related stress and develop locally applicable solutions in partnership with workers. The pack includes: *Tackling Work-Related Stress: a manager's guide to improving and maintaining employee health and well-being*; *Real Solutions, Real People: a manager's guide to tackling work-related stress* (a short introductory guide to the HSE's management standards for stress, to help employers measure their performance in managing stress: this is free leaflet INDG406); *Tackling Work-Related Stress: a guide for employees* (free leaflet INDG341); one A2 action planner; six prompt cards; 18 case study cards; and the Health and Safety Laboratories Research Report 440 *Violence and Aggression Management Training for Trainers and Managers.*

While it is aimed at healthcare sectors, the strategy outlined for combating work-related violence and aggression may be a useful aid to violence management training generally. A complementary practitioner report containing tools and guidance for violence management training is also provided.

The UK's Health and Safety Commission (HSC) – the strategic body for the HSE – is committed to tackling the problem of work-related violence (WRV). In March 2000, the HSC embarked on a three-year programme to help employers tackle WRV, with the aim of reducing the number of incidents of violence at work by the end of 2003.

The HSE has been working with its key stakeholders and partners – from industry, trade unions, local authorities, other government departments and small firms' organizations – to take this programme forward and to help achieve its aims. As part of this programme, the HSE has:

- published case study guidance to help smaller businesses manage the risk of work-related violence, including in the retail sector
- commissioned research to find examples of good practice in preventing and managing violence to lone workers, including in the retail sector
- funded the development of new national occupational standards in the management of work-related violence: these standards were published by the Employment National Training Organization in September 2002, and provide employers with a framework on which to develop detailed policies on WRV.

The HSE hopes that, taken together, the measures in the programme will make a difference to levels of WRV.

The UK HSE has long been concerned about this issue, and has produced a number of publications which give advice and guidance. A free leaflet called *Violence to Staff* (IND (G)69 L) gives practical advice to help you find out if there is a problem, and, if there is, how to tackle it. HSE has also published a priced guidance booklet *Preventing Violence to Staff* that explains the problem-solving process in more detail and includes case studies that show how it can work in practice. The case studies do not involve libraries, but can offer you guidance and advice on how to tackle incidents and problems in any setting.

The HSE's 38-page booklet *Preventing Violence to Retail Staff* gives excellent advice that can be applied to any industry. This guidance booklet will help those developing an in-house policy, and illustrates how to take preventative measures including the training of staff. Another very important area covered is how to give post-incident support to staff, which should not be seen as a separate issue. Providing support for staff should be part of the overall policy on preventing and controlling violence at work. Bear in mind that there is a network of local Victim Support schemes. Victim Support is a national charity providing practical help and information, particularly as regards the criminal justice system (see details in Appendix C).

The number of people working alone is increasing. As organizational downsizing spreads, solitary work is becoming more frequent. The growing practices of sub-contracting, outplacement and teleworking also add to the growth of lone working. In addition, the combined push towards increased mobility and interactive communication technologies encourages the development of one-person operations, for example in a small library. Lone work does not automatically involve a higher risk of violence, but it is generally understood that working alone does increase the vulnerability of workers. This vulnerability will clearly depend on the type of situation in which the lone work is being carried out. The HSE has published more about lone worker violence, including case studies (see www.hse.gov.uk/violence/loneworkcase.htm).

Factors which reduce the effectiveness of preventative measures

The main difficulty with many of the preventative measures described in the published case studies is that they are reliant on individual action: for example, an individual is required to tell someone where they are or to activate an alarm or system, etc. This means that human error or neglect can make even the best system ineffective. Other factors can also reduce the effectiveness of measures, including:

■ lack of attendance at training courses due to pressures of work
■ not carrying a personal alarm within easy reach or knowing how to use it
■ not always being able to avoid potentially violent situations because it goes against a person's 'natural instincts': for example, in a robbery situation, a member of staff might find it difficult to hand over expensive equipment/money without resistance.

Information from violent incidents should be recorded for future reference. Organizations can learn from the experience and knowledge of previous violent incidents and use this to help inform the development of effective strategies to manage work-related violence.

The benefits of violence prevention measures

Libraries and other organizations report many benefits from having measures in place to tackle work-related violence and aggression. These include:

■ a reduction in violent incidents, and in some cases zero incidents being reported
■ improved staff confidence in dealing with violent incidents
■ staff feeling more safe and secure when going about their jobs
■ staff feeling supported and valued by their organization
■ improved working relationships and communication between staff
■ improved customer service
■ reduced staff turnover

■ improved productivity and profitability due to less staff sick leave, improvements in staff efficiency and output, lower recruitment costs, improved library image, etc.

Cost effectiveness of preventative measures

Over the years many organizations have agreed that it is difficult to quantify the costs of violence prevention measures and taken the view that you 'cannot put a price on safety'. While only a small number have carried out an evaluation of their violence measures, all have been able to express a view about their cost effectiveness. Interestingly, some experience an increase in the number of reported incidents following the introduction of violence measures. This can happen when new measures are introduced, because they tend to increase the level of awareness among staff. Generally, organizations report the following:

1 The benefits outweigh the costs. All believe that the benefits of the measures outweigh the costs incurred.
2 The number of reported incidents goes down. Several organizations said that they either had no reported incidents of physical violence or that the number of incidents had recently decreased. However, incidents of verbal abuse often go unreported.
3 A non-confrontational approach costs nothing. Behaving in a polite, helpful and non-aggressive manner does not cost anything.
4 Systems or equipment used in preventative measures are often also used for other business purposes. Many of the violence prevention measures in place are also essential for other aspects of the business, and are therefore cost effective for the organization.
5 Some equipment incurs minimal cost. For some organizations, the cost of equipment and other material (e.g. leaflets/guidance) is minimal compared to the overall income of the organization.
6 Customer/client service shows improvement. Staff feel more happy and confident in their work when they know they have proper support and systems in place to help them deal with potential violence and abuse,

and they are therefore more likely to provide a better service to customers and clients.

7 High technology and high cost security equipment will normally only be needed where there is a particularly high risk of violence.

As we have seen in Chapter 3 'The Business Case', work-related stress is a major cause of occupational ill health – and thus of high staffing costs through sickness absence, high staff turnover and poor staff performance. The HSE has produced management standards to help you, your employees and their representatives manage the issue sensibly and minimize the impact of work-related stress on your business. In fact, it might help you improve organizational performance.

The management standards represent a set of conditions that enable high levels of health, well-being and organizational performance. Following the advice on the HSE website will enable you to identify the gap between your current performance and these conditions. It will also help you to develop your own solutions to close this gap.

Who should use advice on stress management?

Stress management advice is aimed at anyone with responsibility for tackling work-related stress in an organization. This might be the person who has responsibility for co-ordinating your stress risk assessment, human resources managers, health and safety officers, trade union representatives or line managers.

The following HSE publications can help you meet your legal duties. They do not replace HSE's existing stress guidance pack *Real Solutions, Real People* (mentioned on page 53), but provide further practical information, advice and tools on how to assess the risks from work-related stress in your organization: *Management Standards for Tackling Work-related Stress, Short Guide to the Management Standards, Short Guide to the Management Standards* (Welsh language version), and *Overview of the Management Standards Approach* (see www.hse.gov.uk/stress/standards/index.htm for details).

What preventative measures can employees take?

As well as the above, the International Stress Management Association has produced a leaflet *Working Together to Reduce Stress at Work* (www.hse.gov.uk/pubns/misc686.pdf) showing how employees can work with their employers to tackle work-related stress using the management standards approach. The leaflet is supported by the HSE, ACAS, the TUC and the CIPD.

Alternatively, the following measures, originally suggested by The Library Association (now CILIP) in *Violence in Libraries* (The Library Association, 1987), should be considered:

Different people will have different ideas of what is and is not acceptable behaviour, but consistency in this area is vital. Your management should issue a definition of patterns of unacceptable behaviour, listing these in an easily understood way. It is much easier for you and your colleagues to act if you have a clear idea of what should and should not be tolerated.

If you are working in public libraries, the bye-laws could be used and in schools and colleges the institution's rules could be used as a basis for these definitions. The content and status of the bye-laws and rules should be examined for relevance, currency and legality.

If you work in schools, colleges and universities you should investigate whether or not you are legally protected in the same way as the teaching staff when you are in contact with or responsible for groups of children/students.

Make sure that the situation over the right to prosecute is clearly understood by all staff, i.e. can an individual decide to prosecute, or can this only be done by senior management or by elected members?

In cases where offenders are under the age for prosecution, the limitations on taking legal actions should be made known to all staff.

If you have a safety representative in your library or information service, do remember that trade union safety representatives have wide-ranging legal rights under the Safety Representatives and Safety Committees Regulations 1977 to investigate potential problems/hazards, inspect workplaces, speak to members in confidence and take up with employers any complaints about health and safety matters. So it is up to you as an individual to share responsibility for tackling problems or potential problems of aggression, stress and violence in your workplace.

How management can deal with these forms of aggression

Define the problem by producing a policy that clearly states what is and what is not acceptable. This should be produced in consultation with staff groups, unions and managers. These statements must be reviewed annually to ensure that all staff are still content with the information they contain.

Train managers in the appropriate skills – and ensure that these same managers do not bully others. Managers must have people skills, so do not appoint managers who lack these. There is more on training in Chapter 8.

Monitor levels of bullying, complaints and absence – sickness absences may be covering up problems. Watch staff turnover figures and intentions to leave – again, these may be covering up a range of conflict, bullying, stress and harassment situations.

Also, make sure that exit interviews are conducted in such a way that the staff members leaving feel that they can be honest. This may save on recruitment costs in the long term. However, be aware that even leavers may be reluctant to mention anyone specifically involved in bullying. The case studies in Chapter 10 illustrate that sometimes people just leave and know that bullies are, years later, still in their posts and still bullying others.

Offer as many forms of support as possible, both for victims and anyone accused of bullying. This includes using union representatives, managers and personnel/human resources staff. Perhaps all these can help deal with situations before they escalate.

What if your management thinks there is no problem?

Are you sure they understand? Heed the warning: there is no point in looking for trouble where it does not exist, but many problems go unreported for a variety of reasons. Some staff accept troublesome behaviour as part of the job, some see it as a personal failure which they do not wish to admit while some have high rates of tolerance. There is also the very real problem of fear of incidents, rather than the active existence of them.

So do not suffer in silence, but consider making a formal complaint and requesting an investigation.

Any investigation should cover the whole range of aggressive and violent behaviour. You and your colleagues should be consulted to uncover any aggressive or violent incidents in which you have felt threatened or under stress. It is possible that 'isolated incidents' could prove to be more common-place than was previously thought. The initial investigations can be carried out by the personnel department, occupational health nurses, managers, supervisors, trade union representatives or health and safety supervisors. Staff views could be sought via informal interviews or via questionnaires or forms, as suggested in earlier chapters. The answer might still be 'We don't have a problem', and if so then it is still worth pursuing another possibility: putting in place a health and safety management system.

How to get senior management approval for a health and safety management system

You may not be the person responsible for health and safety in your library or organization, but you may already be aware of the risks associated with poor health and safety performance and can see the benefits of implementing a health and safety management system. But implementing a health and safety management system requires time and money. How do you convince your top management that a health and safety management system is worth that investment?

See the earlier sections regarding costs and benefits. The following are a few steps to consider when developing a business case to engage your senior management and gain their commitment to change the culture and make available the resources needed to implement an effective health and safety management system (see also Chapter 3):

1 Carry out a baseline assessment to establish your health and safety performance to date. Provide some statistics on issues such as accidents

and incidents, the number of people having problems with bullying, conflict etc. and absenteeism.

2 Review your existing practices and identify the applicable legal and other health and safety requirements which apply to your library. Establish the likely health and safety hazards and risks associated with normal, abnormal and emergency situations.

3 Define the direction in which you believe your library should be going with regard to health and safety performance. Set the scope of a health and safety management system with some principles, objectives and targets for the future.

4 Point out the benefits of a health and safety management system. More and more legislation is being introduced to manage health and safety. Libraries of any size need to be able to identify, understand and keep on top of legislative requirements. There may be benefits in terms of insurance premiums – all businesses including libraries are looking for ways to reduce their insurance ratings and thus reduce their premiums. And, in extreme cases, implementing a health and safety management system can guard against litigation, protect against copy-cat cases and even protect staff from a potential prison sentence.

5 Estimate the costs of putting a system in place, the resources needed to do so and the costs of external assessment.

There are many people working in information centres and libraries who are suffering, perhaps in silence, from aggression, bullying, harassment and violence. Being aware of the problem, and taking steps to combat it – such as implementing a health and safety management system – will improve the working environment for them and for their colleagues.

POINTS TO REFLECT ON . . .

■ Do you know what is being done to combat aggression and violence by the various authorities?

■ What preventative measures can be taken?

■ Do you know which databases to check for further information?

■ Do you know what to do if your management thinks there is not a problem?

7 Now is the time for you to act!

In this chapter you will find information on:

■ what to do if you and your colleagues *do* have a problem
■ preventative measures, and how to implement and monitor them.

Previous chapters have outlined the range of legislation in place to minimize workplace stress and violence, the range of publications that can help you, the organizational costs and benefits of health and safety measures, and how to assess and manage risks and build a business case for a health and safety system. This chapter tells you what you and your colleagues and managers can do – starting right now – to address a problem and prevent it from re-occurring.

What to do if you and your colleagues *do* have a problem

Information regarding the problem needs to be collated and analysed, but there are situations where the process of data gathering and analysis will be too slow, and action will need to be taken urgently. There must be an emergency route direct to a manager who has the authority to take immediate action, which should be written into any anti-harassment policy statement.

Data collection

The HSE suggests that if a problem is identified, then a formal reporting system should be established, as a first step. For this you need a purpose-designed form similar to the widely used incident report forms (see Figure 7.1). Some authorities have also introduced monthly summary forms. Responsibility for the collection and analysis of this information could rest with health and safety supervisors or with managers. It is important that *all* staff are made aware of the proper reporting channels.

Data analysis

When the information has been collected it should be analysed to see whether particular kinds of incident are more common than others. These incidents need to be grouped together into types, each of which will have its own identifying pattern – for example, harassment from rowdy groups when on late duty. It is through this type of data gathering that particularly vulnerable jobs or tasks can be identified and a search for preventative measures can begin. If you and your colleagues can suggest some solutions then you should inform your managers.

Preventative measures
Management attitude

It is probable that your managers will employ a mixture of preventative measures to achieve control and manage the problem effectively. It is important that these are appropriate and adequate for the task, and that they are cost-effective. Staff need to be aware of them and trained where appropriate. Installing expensive security hardware, for instance, without changing inadequate systems and procedures is not likely to be sufficient. Your managers will also need to consider whether the preventative measures could increase the possibility of violence.

The attitude of managers towards a potential problem can drastically affect the reactions of staff and their ability to cope with difficult situations.

Date of incident	Day of the week	Time
EMPLOYEE		
Name		
Library workplace		
Telephone number		
E-mail		
Supervisor/Manager		
Telephone number		
E-mail		
What activity were you engaged in at the time of the incident?		
CIRCUMSTANCES OF INCIDENT		
Was assault physical or verbal?		
Location		
Number of other staff present		
Was medical assistance/ first aid required?		
Was sick leave required?		
Injury or stress suffered		
Time lost		
Legal action		
WHAT HAPPENED		
Give brief details of incident, including any relevant events leading to the incident. Injury? Verbal abuse/shouting? Anti-social behaviour? Damage to personal property/other property?		
Give brief details of assailant (approximate age, height, condition, etc.)		
Near any CCTV?		
Has assailant been involved in any previous incident?	YES	NO
Give date and brief details		

Figure 7.1 Typical reporting form

The old Library Association leaflet (see page 59) suggested:

> A written statement showing sympathy and understanding and containing positive information, e.g. on insurance protection, can boost the confidence of staff in direct contact with the public. This can be expanded into a 'Help' leaflet, or guidance notes, to be circulated to *all* staff.

Examples of these can be obtained from a search of library websites, especially libraries in universities.

Communication and consultation

The reporting procedure has been mentioned already but the importance of effective two-way communication cannot be stressed enough.

You must feel able to discuss problems with managers, and managers must consult with staff and trade union representatives at all stages. Some authorities have established working parties to investigate the problem, which have produced reporting forms and from the results have made recommendations to senior management or local authority committees. These working parties can include training officers, union representatives, crime prevention officers, community police officers and staff at various levels.

Good working relationships

There are many examples to be seen, in various communities, where good working relationships with a number of groups have been established to help alleviate problems. Contacts with teachers, headteachers and governors at schools, with police, youth leaders and probation officers, and with other types of library and other organizations within the community may be beneficial, enabling a discussion of the problems, an exchange of information and a co-ordinated approach. There could be scope for a committee to include other community workers, meeting either on a regular or an ad hoc basis. Some libraries have formed user committees, which have made a positive contribution to this and other issues.

Informal contact with local police officers can be more productive, and if officers are made aware of the contents of bye-laws etc. they will be better equipped to deal with incidents which they might otherwise regard as outside the remit of the law.

Mediation

It can often seem easier to avoid conflict and hope it will go away, but that is how problems escalate. When you are involved in conflict, a solution may seem impossible. You may not even be able to talk to the person you are in conflict with because things have become so fraught. ACAS says:

> As can be seen in many employment tribunal sessions the incident started with a small spark, e.g. conflict between staff members or an employee with a problem not taken seriously or a badly handled discipline interview or a misunderstanding between people which was then fanned into a flame and finally erupted into a volcano. Help from someone independent and even-handed like ACAS may be the only way things can be improved.

Mediation is:

- a way of sorting out disagreements or disputes without having to go to court: a neutral third person works with those in disagreement or dispute to help them reach an agreement that will sort out their problems
- voluntary: you only take part if you want to
- confidential: nothing you say will be passed on to anyone else unless you agree and nothing said in mediation can be used in any later company procedures or court action.

The aim is to maintain the employment relationship if at all possible. Mediation is about the future, not the past and who was right or wrong.

Working environment considerations

The way your workplace is designed and laid out might help to prevent incidents of aggression and violence. Crime prevention officers will advise on the security of existing buildings and – an often overlooked point – on the design of new buildings. A number of organizations have found the following measures decrease the possibility of violence:

- providing clear visibility and lighting for staff so that they can either leave quickly or they can raise help: ensuring that lighting is adequate both inside and outside the building and in car parks might also help to identify potential assailants, as will making sure that car parks are not too isolated from the information centre/library
- considering the effects of the locality of the library/information centre: a building shared with other community services with different opening times, near a youth club or psychiatric unit, or in an area known for disturbances, may create some problems for staff and its users
- ensuring that inside the building all parts of the information centre/library can be seen and that the windows can be seen through
- ensuring that staff entrances and exits are safe, particularly for those who are working late: safety equipment such as video surveillance cameras may be needed (this is particularly necessary for staff such as caretakers and cleaners, who are often in the building outside normal opening hours)
- considering the use of alarms, panic buttons and walkie-talkies, and training staff, including security staff, how to react to an emergency
- positioning cash tills away from customers and/or providing physical security at cash tills
- ensuring that the minimum necessary cash and build-up of cash is kept in tills by adopting procedures to move cash quickly and safely to more secure zones
- widening counters and/or raising counter heights on the staff side to give staff more protection (some pubs have done this); relocating the counter if it is in the wrong place; ensuring that the public cannot get behind the counter
- ensuring adequate queue management by using clear and ample signs and, where appropriate, ensuring easy access

- arranging for staff to have access to a secure location and a secure place for personal possessions
- changing the layout of any public areas by providing better seating, lighting and decor
- providing bright lighting around the building and removing possible cover for assailants targeting staff leaving the building after late duties
- ensuring good quality control on services and systems to defuse any possibility of aggression; providing regular information about any delays
- monitoring high-risk entrances, exits and delivery points.

Before an expensive redesign of your library or information centre is undertaken, management will need to make sure that it is appropriate to the risk and is relevant to the needs of your work.

There are many ways of making improvements and it is worth examining your physical environment with a critical eye.

Job design considerations

The way jobs are designed can reduce the risk of violence. But there are no ready-made remedies; you will have to find measures that are right for your workplace. Here are some examples of measures that have worked for some organizations.

- changing the job to give less face-to-face contact with the public (care should be taken that such measures do not increase the risks of violence to members of the public because there are no visible staff)
- using cheques, credit cards or tokens instead of cash to make robbery less attractive
- checking the credentials of 'clients' and if possible the place and arrangements for meetings away from the office (this is now standard practice for some estate agents)
- monitoring staffing levels, as even in times of financial constraint it may be necessary to increase staffing levels so that one person is not left alone, especially in the evenings (alterations in hours can allow this to happen without the need to increase numbers of staff, or security

officers may be employed or hired from specialist firms)
- ensuring that staff can get home safely, as the threat of violence does not stop when work has ended: the Health and Safety at Work etc. Act requires employers to protect employees while they are at work, but good employers will take further steps where necessary (for example, many organizations arrange transport to take their staff home if late hours are required)
- training should be offered, both to give staff more knowledge and confidence in their particular jobs, and to enable them to deal with aggression generally by spotting the early signs of it, by avoiding it or by coping with it
- installing video cameras: on buses, for example, cameras have protected staff and reduced vandalism and graffiti
- putting protective screens around staff areas, as in some banks, social security offices and bus drivers' cabs
- adding coded security locks to doors to keep the public out of staff areas.

Staff in mobile libraries may experience particular difficulties in implementing some of the above measures, and should be involved in discussions when security is being considered so that their points of view can be assimilated.

Working procedures

Revising your working procedures or introducing new methods might help to prevent incidents of violence to staff. Again, a number of organizations have found various measures which are beneficial. These include:

- ensuring that staffing levels are appropriate to the particular task and the time of day, and, if there is a high risk, ensuring the level is adequate to the risk
- providing adequate and appropriate information to staff on procedures and systems
- ensuring that customer care programmes are adequately designed and managed; this will be particularly appropriate for dealing with complaints

■ including specific training on violence to staff as part of the health and safety management training programme (see Chapter 6)

■ establishing clear emergency procedures, for example training for staff in what to do and where to go in the event of an incident, providing emergency telephone numbers, etc.

■ if cash is taken to the bank, varying the times when it is taken and changing the route: consideration could be given to using professional cash collection services

■ ensuring that experienced or less vulnerable staff are used for high-risk tasks

■ rotating high-risk jobs so that the same person is not always at risk, or doubling up for particularly high-risk tasks

■ providing additional staff for high-risk mobile activities or providing communication links to base

■ ensuring that planned staff schedules are held by the base

■ providing transport for staff who work alone

■ providing personal alarms for high-risk staff

■ providing training in recognizing and dealing with violence, and the potential for violence.

Security systems and procedures

These will generally include security equipment specifically designed to prevent or deter violent crime. A decision will need to be made about whether such equipment is appropriate to the risk. There is no point in buying expensive and sophisticated CCTV systems if the risk is minimal. Creating an environment where security is excessive and impractical should be avoided.

The level and design of equipment will need to take into account:

■ ease of use by staff

■ the pattern and type of business

■ the way the building is used

■ whether the geographical location is urban or rural, as this may affect the local crime rate: find out what the experience of other businesses in the area is

■ the need for emergency access/control.

If you do not have in-house security expertise, you may wish to contact your local police crime prevention officer for advice.

You and your colleagues will feel that the organization is taking a caring attitude towards you if help is given in various forms as described above, and the following may also help:

■ practical training in how to operate and maintain the security equipment: after all, the equipment will only be as effective as the staff trained to use it
■ practice in the skills involved in any specific security duties held: this will help to build up confidence in the system.

Certain aspects of security procedures should be treated as highly confidential. These details should be given out on a 'need-to-know' basis only. This will help to contain the risk of violence. However, all staff, including part-time or casual workers, will need training in some aspects of security. It may also be useful to display notices so that the public are aware that certain security devices are used in the information centre or library.

Items of equipment such as alarms will need regular maintenance checks to ensure that they are reliable and effective. You and your colleagues will also wish to monitor and evaluate systems to confirm that they are still appropriate. But before your management installs new security equipment to deal with a new threat, consider how it relates to your old security systems.

Implementation

Many of the measures outlined above can be implemented with little or no financial outlay, and put into practice within a short timescale. Other measures have larger financial implications and should be incorporated into a rolling programme with appropriate allowance within the budget.

Trades union/staff consultation is crucial at the planning, implementation and monitoring stages.

Monitoring

It is essential that the effect of each measure is monitored properly. Effective measures can be identified and sustained; less effective ones can be replaced or modified. Changes in behaviour patterns can be assessed and policies changed accordingly.

Effective monitoring can also be a valuable method of staff reassurance: if it can be seen that measures are effective, staff morale will be boosted.

POINTS TO REFLECT ON . . .

- Do you know what to do if you and your colleagues *do* have a problem?
- Do you know how to investigate whether a problem exists?
- What preventative measures can be taken?
- What type of reporting procedures do you know about?
- Do you know how to check that procedures work?

8 Dealing with aggression and violence

In this chapter you will find information on:

■ steps to improve your personal safety

■ actually dealing with all forms of aggression

■ what could be included in staff guidelines for dealing with an incident

■ training

■ networking

■ counselling arrangements.

Steps to improve your personal safety

There are various ways in which you can train yourself to deal with difficult situations and develop communication skills and assertiveness. Remember to look confident (even if you do not feel it) because a confident-looking person is less likely to be attacked. You should also keep fit; exercise can help you develop posture, stamina and strength.

Try at all times to avoid confrontation and learn how to do all you can to defuse a potentially violent situation. Should you feel scared or uneasy, act on it straight away and if at all possible move away as confidently and quickly as possible. Should you find yourself in danger, your primary aim is to get away fast, avoiding violence.

Also, be prepared to help if you see someone else in danger. If at all possible carry a personal telephone with you and make sure that it is charged up!

If necessary telephone for assistance using your organization's emergency number or 999.

Safety when on the move

Sometimes your work can take you to new or unfamiliar locations: going on training courses, working at another branch of the information service, or attending a conference or a meeting. Make sure someone knows where you are. Leave your schedule behind – train/bus times, hotel name, address, telephone number, etc. Know exactly where you are going and how to get there. If your travel plans change, tell your supervisor/colleagues. Make sure you can be contacted. Do you or your organization check out beforehand the people you meet alone?

If travelling home after dark, consider all possible risks (e.g. where you parked the car, the availability of public transport, whether anyone is meeting you, etc.). Avoid carrying cash or valuable items. Make sure that valuable items are not too visible or accessible (e.g. laptop computer, mobile phone, briefcase or handbag). Think about carrying a personal alarm or mobile telephone.

EMERGENCY NUMBER IN THE UK

DIAL 999 – THE CALL IS FREE OF CHARGE

When calling the emergency number give as much information as possible, including the following:

- **Nature of the incident**
- **Location of the incident**
- **Type and seriousness of injuries, if any**

Remember the following:

- **Keep calm, speak clearly and do not hang up until the emergency services have *all* the information needed**
- **Don't wait until an emergency arises – be trained and able to react correctly**
- **No policy or precautions can guarantee the safety of every individual in every situation.**

Safety when working alone at your usual workplace

If it is necessary to undertake late-night duties or weekend work, will you be working alone? Consider whether there are areas where you feel uneasy (e.g. poorly lit entrances or corridors, car parks, etc.), and whether your office/work area might be a potential trap (e.g. is a possible escape route blocked by a desk, filing cabinet, bookshelves, counter etc.?).

If you work in a large organization with security staff on 24-hour duty, inform them that you are working late and what time you expect to finish.

Learn to be an effective communicator

Formal training may be necessary to make you an effective communicator, which will help you to reduce considerably the risk of aggressive or potentially violent situations developing. Bear in mind that it is well known that communication is not just verbal – up to 90% of communication between individuals is nonverbal.

If you are experiencing some form of aggression or bullying from clients or colleagues, work to placate rather than provoke them. Learn to talk your way out of problems and, if this fails, call upon others to help. *Do not suffer in silence* or you will find yourself becoming tense and stressed, which in itself may increase the other person's aggression.

Useful safety tips

As we have already seen in various examples in this book, it is apparent that aggression, bullying, conflict, harassment and violence in the workplace is on the increase. Here are a number of useful guidelines you might incorporate on a daily basis:

- Avoid actions which may appear aggressive or may be perceived as an invasion of privacy, e.g. in the desk or work area avoid reading papers or taking any equipment without asking first.
- Avoid standing too close/touching someone you work with and avoid over-familiar talk or lewd suggestions.
- Do not give your own or colleagues' home telephone numbers or

addresses to customers, or anyone else, unless there is an agreement to do so. Also, if working in public areas, do not give your personal telephone number when on the telephone, because you do not know who else is listening to you!

■ If anyone in a lift makes you feel uneasy, avoid eye contact, look confident, be on the alert and get out at the next floor.

■ It should be possible to avoid after-hours meetings if you are on your own but, if they are unavoidable, ensure that someone knows where you are.

■ You can dress to please yourself, but bear in mind that society has unwritten rules about appropriate dress for most occupations and situations, so wear clothes which give out the signals you intend.

■ Never get into a car with somebody you do not know and trust.

Actually dealing with all forms of aggression

Aggression as defined earlier in the book by various organizations may include verbal abuse, ostracism, discrimination, racial or sexual harassment, bullying, etc. You need to be able to assess a situation and decide quickly what actions you should take to contain and curtail this aggression. Training should show you how to deal with a variety of situations, even those that could lead to physical attack. Refer to Chapter 1 for a list of the various types of behaviour that might be considered offensive, and the informal and formal procedures that might be used to deal with them.

It will be necessary to learn not to respond in kind, even if someone is trying to provoke you. Meeting aggression with aggression leads to confrontation and someone could get hurt. At all times you must stay calm and speak gently, slowly and clearly. Do not argue or try to outsmart the person verbally. Breathe slowly to control your own tension. Learn how to avoid body language which may be misinterpreted, such as looking down on the aggressor; placing hands on hips, folding or raising your arms or using any physical contact. It is advisable to keep your distance.

Also, try to talk through the problem and, however angry you may feel, try to get the person to see your manager or another colleague. If possible, allow the person's aggression to be diverted against inanimate objects, such as kicking the library counter. Promote compromise by offering the aggressor a way out of the situation.

If you cannot deflect or defuse the situation, then get away as quickly and safely as possible. While the incident is taking place keep talking and assess possible ways of escaping if the situation worsens. Try to prevent the aggressor blocking any possible escape route. Never turn your back. If you are trying to get away, move gradually backwards.

After the incident, do learn from it and protect yourself and others from repeated aggressive behaviour. You must therefore report the incident to your immediate supervisor and ensure that your complaint is taken seriously and receives a fair hearing. Fill in the incident form (see the example on page 65).

Physical attack

If you are threatened, you must try not to freeze up but to get away as fast as you can. Aim for a place where you know there will be people, either in your information centre or library or outside. Do not look back, and report the incident immediately to the police. Someone else might be attacked and may not be able to get away.

If it is not possible to get away, protect yourself and sound your personal alarm if you have one. Shout or scream and give the command 'Phone the police!' or a similar positive instruction – people are more likely to react when given a call to action.

As a last resort, the police advice is 'bash and dash'. If you have to fight back, do it quickly. Aim for the knee, solar plexus, elbow joint or little fingers. Then get away.

It is safer to carry a personal alarm than an offensive weapon, which could be used against you.

Self-defence

During your training you will learn that physical self-defence should only be used as the last resort because it limits your options for getting away and will invariably commit you to a fight that you could well lose. Remember also that if you respond physically you could be legally liable for assault.

Staff guidelines for dealing with an incident

Your management's health and safety policy should give you guidelines about what is acceptable behaviour at work and tell you how to report any incidents. Even after successful implementation of preventative measures, it is inevitable that incidents will still happen, and the health and safety guidelines should include information to help staff when situations do flare up. The following are suggestions for inclusion in the guidelines to be given to all staff:

- Do not over-react. However, do not wait until situations get worse. Act decisively and positively.
- Try to remain calm.
- Do not argue or threaten.
- Avoid simple mistakes like blocking the exit when asking people to leave.
- If you threaten to call the police, call them.
- Identify troublemakers and learn their names, and tell other colleagues who may have to deal with them on other occasions.
- Explain why their actions are unacceptable.
- Managers should also decide whether persistent troublemakers should be banned, the exact procedure for making the ban effective and how to inform all concerned.
- Managers should clarify under what circumstances staff have the right to close the premises.
- All staff should follow the reporting procedure.

Investigations into the problem of aggression and violence at work and its solutions should be carried out continually as part of ongoing risk assessment. You should be aware of the valuable work being done by many trade unions and bodies like the Tavistock Institute of Human Relations. A number of other organizations who can provide help and support are listed in Appendix C.

Training

Training will be an important element in managing and preventing the risk of aggression and violence to staff and should be used:

- to brief you and your colleagues on your organization's policy and procedures
- to deliver advice, information and skills on prevention
- to involve you and your colleagues in sharing experiences and thoughts on the subject
- as a catalyst to bring about change within your workplace.

CILIP's Training and Development Department organizes training courses and workshops on coping with violence and aggression in libraries, as do Victim Support and other organizations (see Appendix C for further details of these organizations). Watch the professional press for details of courses and seminars.

Training topics

Changes in risks may require changes in the content of training (e.g. where new procedures have been introduced). Health and safety training should take place during working hours. If it is necessary to arrange training outside your normal hours, this should be treated as an extension of time at work.

Training on prevention might include:

- detailing policies for and systems of dealing with the problems
- recognizing and dealing with abusive and aggressive customers, who may display irrational behaviour, nervousness or hostility, avoid eye contact and take an aggressive stance
- exploring the causes of violence and aggression, such as anger and frustration
- explaining to staff what to do and what is expected of them in the event of aggression, violence and assault including, for example, how to raise the alarm, where to go for safety and not to resist or follow violent offenders

■ managing confrontation by using positive interpersonal skills such as listening, remaining calm and confident, being assertive rather than aggressive, defusing situations before they escalate by being non-confrontational and offering a compromise, attracting the attention of colleagues and, if all else fails, ensuring an escape route

■ ensuring effective handling of incidents by letting staff know what to do and who to tell; also giving advice on the degree of risk involved and using role-play to help staff feel comfortable and confident about security equipment (e.g. panic alarms)

■ providing effective customer care by being polite, calm and helpful, and recognizing the other person's point of view

■ ensuring safe working practices; if staff are mobile this involves ensuring that someone at the fixed workplace is aware of their exact movements, and for all staff this involves avoiding, where possible, working alone or in isolation

■ providing support and care after the incident, including dealing with the impact it can have on staff and making arrangements for support (this will be particularly appropriate for managers and supervisors).

The managers of each department/branch will have a key role in identifying the training needs of you and other staff. In particular, managers are tasked with controlling and preventing risk. Thus managers must be provided with sufficient training on the issue to become competent in the management role (this could be part of general management training). Managers may need to consider specific training if you or colleagues move from low-risk to high-risk tasks. All of you will need to be thoroughly briefed on areas of concern to help reduce any foreseeable risk. Where safety representatives are appointed, these should be consulted on training issues.

You should also be aware that training needs in your organization should be monitored and reviewed regularly, and training courses should be evaluated for their effectiveness. Remember, even if you are a part-time worker you will still need the same training as full-time members of staff.

You and all your colleagues will need to be aware of any risk which you could face while carrying out the job – for example during shift working, mobile work, etc. Being aware of and able to recognize the potential danger will help you to be prepared, and enable you to react to a situation in a positive way, because you know what could happen and what would be the best way to deal with it. Training in awareness will include examples of good practice in recognizing and responding to risky situations. It will also provide you with practical knowledge and information on preventative measures (e.g. systems, procedures and equipment). Awareness can often help to avoid incidents, although it will not always guarantee prevention. Violent incidents will and do happen.

If your management has a policy on apprehending criminals, you and your colleagues will need adequate training and information to ensure that you always act within the law in doing so.

Training at all levels should be paramount in all libraries and information centres, especially in health and safety matters that encompass the well-being of staff. It is an important way of achieving competence and helps to convert information into safe working practice. It contributes to your organization's health and safety culture and is needed at all levels, including top management. Risk assessment is required under the terms of the Management of Health and Safety at Work Regulations 1992 Statutory Instrument 1992 No. 2051, and will help to determine the level of training needed for each type of work undertaken. This may include basic skills training, specific on-the-job training and training in health and safety or emergency procedures for each type of work.

Training needs are likely to be greatest on recruitment. If you are a new employee you should receive basic induction training on health and safety, including arrangements for first aid, fire and evacuation. Your organization should also pay particular attention to the needs of young workers. The risk assessment process should indicate further specific training needs. In some cases, training may be required even though an employee already holds formal qualifications.

Changes in your work environment may cause you to be exposed to new or increased risks, and to require further training. Further training should be considered when you or your colleagues transfer or take on new responsibilities, and/or there is a change in the work or in the work environment (this could include staffing changes). Training may also be needed if there is a change in the work equipment or systems of work in use.

A significant change is likely to need a review and re-assessment of the risks, which may indicate additional training needs. If the change includes introducing completely new technology, it may bring with it new and unfamiliar tasks. Competent outside advice may be needed.

Know the health and safety issues regarding aggression, bullying, conflict, harassment, stress and violence in your workplace. Everyone needs to become more confident about dealing with it and about being able to identify the types and triggers of violent aggressive behaviour. Staff need to be able to recognize and understand how their own body language and methods of communication can affect others. Everyone needs to realize that defusing and de-escalating situations is by far the best way of dealing with such incidents.

Management and representatives who may be involved in grievance matters should be trained for the task. They should be familiar with the provisions of the grievance procedure, and know how to conduct or represent at grievance hearings. Where trade unions are recognized, consideration might be given to training managers and trade union representatives jointly.

Record-keeping

Keeping records is a health and safety investigation requirement, and is part of health and safety training. Any records written and maintained should be treated as confidential and kept in accordance with the Data Protection Act 1998, which gives individuals the right to request and have access to certain personal data.

The overriding principles of the Data Protection Act 1998 are that any personal data kept should be necessary, fairly and lawfully processed, adequate, relevant, accurate and secure. Clearly, records of grievance matters should only be kept if they adhere to these principles, and the parties involved should be assured of their accuracy and confidentiality. The Information Commissioner has published codes of practice covering recruitment and selection, employment records, monitoring at work and medical information (visit www.ico.gov.uk).

Refresher training

Your competence will decline if your skills (e.g. in emergency procedures) are not practised regularly. Training therefore needs to be repeated periodically to ensure continued competence. Information from personal performance monitoring, health and safety checks, accident investigations and near-miss incidents can help to establish a suitable time lag before retraining.

If you occasionally deputize for others, consider whether you need training in any safety procedures. Your skills are likely to be under-developed and you may need more frequent refresher training.

Networking

Networking with other libraries or information centres in your area will enable you to pool knowledge and experience and share information on best practice. It will also help to build a safer working community. It may be that, by networking with similar information services in your area, you and your management are able to set up crime prevention initiatives. Links could also be formed with local commerce and trade associations.

Lessons can be learned from sharing information about styles of management, strategies, systems and the skills required to underpin them. Violence to staff should be a concern to everyone in the area: it could affect you. Depending on the size of your organization, networking can also be useful at regional and national levels. It will, however, be important to agree ground rules for sharing information when it relates to particular security measures used by specific libraries or information centres.

Networking could also provide a means of support for anyone who is a victim of a serious violent incident. It helps to prevent isolation and encourages members of the network to work together in improving the crime rate. Larger libraries will be in a good position to set standards and help those which may have fewer resources and less information available to them. Crime and violent incidents become rapidly known in a locality, and are often used to judge what the area is like to live and work in. Positive efforts for the community could lead to an improved and safer working environment, and increased profits for local businesses.

The crime prevention officer and the local authority environmental health department will be able to provide you with further information on local crime prevention initiatives and security measures. Some local authorities have crime prevention working groups with councillor representation and involvement. Local Victim Support schemes will also be able to offer their support and information to staff.

Counselling arrangements

It is essential that counselling must be available for all staff immediately after violent incidents. See Chapter 9 for details.

Note

Please note that the information given here is no substitute for training, procedures and practice.

POINTS TO REFLECT ON . . .

■ Do you think about the risks at work?

■ Can you suggest some improvements (even minor changes) to current practice and procedure?

■ Be vigilant and assess possible risks in your everyday work life, from when you leave home to when you return.

■ If an incident occurs which requires police assistance, do you know what to do?

■ Have you had any training in dealing with aggression and violence?

9

Support you can expect after an incident

In this chapter you will learn about:

■ what you can expect from grievance procedures
■ what help a victim may need
■ the immediate support you can expect
■ the longer-term support.

Introduction

We saw in earlier chapters that your employer's overall health and safety policy should include details of responses to staff after an incident involving any form of aggression. Every effort should be made to help minimize and control the impact on staff, and to ensure that they recover from the incident as soon as possible.

It can often be clear (especially in the case studies in Chapter 10) that management in many cases does not want to 'rock the boat' and will not accept that anything is going wrong in their workplace. Hence, it is necessary for the health and safety policy to identify the staff with principal responsibilities at each stage, so that all staff members are informed of their role and, more importantly, what they should do in case of such incidents.

Using the grievance procedure

When an incident involves two members of staff, or when an incident involving a member of staff and a member of the public is not dealt with satisfactorily, the library's grievance procedure can be followed in an attempt to bring the matter to closure as completely as possible for those concerned.

The library's grievance procedure should be written down and should specify who should be contacted. Sometimes it is better for the people involved to be brought together to discuss the situation before it escalates into days, months and perhaps years of agony for members of staff. The Commission for Racial Equality advice in the Statutory Code of Practice on racial equality in employment states:

Grievance procedure

An arrangement or procedure for dealing with grievances about practice or conduct in the workplace, such as bullying or harassment or racial discrimination, or appeals against decisions on promotion or, in some cases, appraisal marks. From October 2004, under the Employment Act 2002, employees must invoke a statutory grievance procedure if they wish subsequently to use the grievance as the basis of certain applications to an employment tribunal.

This does not mean that the procedure should only be used by potential tribunal applicants.

The ACAS Code of Practice on Disciplinary and Grievance Procedures provides detailed guidance for employers. ACAS advises that it is better to deal with conflict at an early stage because it saves you stress and has a better chance of success. The first thing to do is to talk things over with your employer, but if that does not sort things out ACAS can help in all sorts of ways:

■ You can telephone the ACAS helpline on 08457 47 47 47 and they will give you practical advice on dealing with different employment issues.
■ ACAS can inform you about the minimum statutory grievance and disciplinary procedures (although you will also need to make sure you know about your library's procedures for handling these matters).
■ ACAS may be able to arrange mediation for you; there is a charge for this help.

See also the ACAS publications *Code of Practice – Disciplinary and Grievance Procedures ACAS/CP01* and *Producing Disciplinary and Grievance Procedures (ACAS/G02)*, available through www.acas.org.uk.

This code aims to help employers, workers and their representatives by giving practical advice on how to deal with grievances and disciplinary actions, and guiding them through the decision-making process. ACAS has also produced a number of other publications, including *Bullying and Harassment at Work* (ACAS, 2007) and *Managing Attendance and Employee Turnover* (ACAS, 2006).

What about the victims?

Victims may need help. From employers this may include counselling, time off and/or help with compensation and legal advice. From work colleagues it may mean giving evidence in court, talking about problems or just being sensitive to the victim's feelings and providing support.

It is useful to be clear about the support you plan to give before an attack happens. Employees will be better able to cope with stressful situations once they know they have their management's support.

If criminal proceedings ensue, the Home Office Victim Support website (www.homeoffice.gov.uk/crime-victims/victims/victim-support/) gives information about the variety of help available. This includes Victim Support, which is an independent national charity with staff and volunteers in regional offices who are specially trained to provide victims with free emotional support and practical assistance, including:

- someone to talk to in confidence
- advice on victims' rights
- information on police and court procedures
- advice about compensation and insurance
- links to other sources of help, e.g. counselling.

Anyone affected by crime can contact Victim Support for help, regardless of whether they have reported the crime to the police or how long ago the crime took place. Your employer may be able to seek help with training in risk management from the local crime prevention officer. Victim Support will be able to assist with training and providing help and information to staff.

Victim Support helps victims of crime in England, Wales and Northern Ireland. There is a separate organization for Scotland. The service is confidential and free. Victim Support can provide someone to accompany the victim/witness to court if requested. These services are being developed through court-based services in Crown Court centres. The Witness Service offers information and support before, during and after a trial in close liaison with local Victim Support schemes and criminal justice agencies. (See Appendix C for details about how to contact Victim Support.)

Reactions to an incident

When an act of aggression or violence happens it is always a frightening experience because it is unpredictable; the impact on the victim's physical and psychological health can be longlasting and may not immediately be apparent. Consequently support, care and counselling may be needed to help recovery.

Staff may find themselves reacting in various ways which can lead to inefficiency and low morale as well as stress. All these may not be apparent at the time of the incident but may manifest themselves later, and supervisors need to be on the alert to help the victims.

It is possible that staff will feel anxious about working late, or alone, or will not want to deal with customers known to be awkward or difficult. There is always the fear of assailants or aggressors returning or, worse, waiting for staff to finish work and then following them.

You and colleagues may feel frustrated, angry and helpless and experience loss of confidence and concentration. Some staff are so badly affected that these reactions persist, affecting both their personal and professional lives. The main thing is for colleagues, friends and management to be aware that anyone involved in, or at the receiving end of, aggression and violence will need support.

Training can be helpful for lessening shock; managers will need basic training in dealing with staff during and immediately after an incident. Support and understanding are the key factors in helping staff to recover from a traumatic event. Managers and colleagues will need to understand the impact of shock and how to handle it. They will need the support of the senior managers on site, and they will need practical operational help if they are expected to keep the information centre or library open.

What to do after an incident has occurred

Some action is necessary as soon as possible after an incident. In addition to private discussion with the victim, an informal group meeting of all those involved peripherally or affected by the incident, or individual conversations with an appointed member of staff, may be appropriate. This type of support does not have to be a sophisticated response – sometimes a simple chat and an assessment made that nothing further is needed may be all that is necessary. An immediate response to needs will help staff feel that what they are going through is a normal reaction and that this need for support is not seen as a failure on their part.

Sometimes group discussions can be particularly effective for sharing experience, concerns and feelings. They can help to ensure that staff do not feel isolated and are aware that there are others with similar reactions and fears. Group discussions can involve those who are directly or indirectly affected. However, their success depends on the willingness of everyone to take part.

It is vital that there is a key person involved with the team who is supportive and has an understanding of the likely impact on individuals. An effective, sensitive initial response is crucial to people's ability to cope in the longer term. It is essential to avoid a situation where staff suffer a loss of self-esteem and are unable to undertake certain tasks or duties. Staff should be given the opportunity to express their feelings and be given:

■ an outline of the incident (subject to the approval of the victim)
■ a report on the progress of any investigation or action taken by the management and the police, including what is likely to happen next
■ decisions about whether special leave is to be allowed to enable recovery from the incident (this may need to be balanced with encouraging staff to return to 'normality')

■ legal advice and help in taking proceedings against the assailant.

You and your colleagues should be given what help is needed: emotional support and practical help including, if necessary, the rearranging of duties/rosters.

Learning from the feedback about experiences is often helpful in avoiding a recurrence and should be incorporated into the management's policies and action plans.

Follow-up action should be taken after a period of time (probably around a month after the incident) to ensure that staff have recovered and do not require additional help. Information and further guidance could also be given about any police action taken: if appropriate, staff will need to be prepared for an eventual court case. Victim Support offers help here and it is worth consulting them.

Long-term support

It is possible that some staff will require extra help and time to overcome their fear, anger and stress, which cannot be provided in the initial response. This should be assessed at follow-up sessions and it may be that counselling or retraining is appropriate.

Should counselling be undertaken in-house it will be important that it is seen to be an independent and confidential service, tailored to individual circumstances and individual staff. Otherwise a victim will not feel confident in discussing highly personal and possibly distressing experiences. Counsellors will need to have first-class interpersonal skills: communicating, listening, empathizing, objectivity, tolerance and recognition. It should not be assumed that every member of staff has these qualities; again, Victim Support can help and provide the services needed.

If you are the victim, there are other steps to consider to enable you to survive such ordeals:

■ Make an appointment with your doctor and tell him/her what is happening to you at work.
■ Follow medical instructions and get signed off if necessary.

- If counselling is available at work make an early appointment to talk through your experience.
- If no workplace counselling is available then check to see if your medical practice has a counselling service. If not, then find a service in your area.
- Make a conscious effort to eat a well balanced diet.
- Learn to relax (this might be difficult).
- Maintain contact with friends outside work. You will need a good listener.
- Make time to do the things you enjoy outside work.
- Get in touch with the Andrea Adams Trust (see Appendix C) or a similar organization that can advise and support you.

Police action

If the incident is considered to have involved a criminal act, a nominated staff member should immediately contact the police. The reporting procedure should enable a detailed description of the event, offender(s), injuries etc. to be fully covered.

Local police stations will also know how to contact the nearest Victim Support scheme. If there are none locally (double-check your telephone book first), contact the national headquarters (see Appendix C). You will also find useful guidance in the HSE booklet *Preventing Violence to Staff* (HSE, 1995a).

HSE management standards

Remember that your library or organization should be giving as much support as possible to victims of aggression, bullying, conflict, harassment and violence. As already mentioned, HSE has defined management standards that outline the characteristics or culture of an organization that manages stress effectively (see Chapter 5 and also www.hse.gov.uk/stress/standards).

Identifying necessary improvements following an incident

You may also wish to consider the questions in the following list when you are trying to make improvements to your library or workplace after an incident. This may also bring to light that all is not well in other departments or units of the library. Staff members could be asked:

- Do you have control over
  - your workload?
  - how fast you work?
  - when you start and finish work?
  - when you take breaks?
- Do you get support from your supervisor or line manager?
- Do you have the privacy you need at work?
- Have you been given the training necessary for your current job?
- Do you have a chance to develop your skills through training or advancement in your job?
- Do you have a chance to use your creativity at work?
- Do you have an opportunity to influence decisions which affect you as an individual?
- Are you allowed to meet with other workers to discuss decisions affecting you?

Making further improvements in your workplace

Many libraries and organizations have anti-harassment policies and procedures for staff. For a full example see the University of Glasgow's *Harassment Policy and Procedures for Staff*, which rather usefully has a list of named Volunteer Harassment Officers with telephone numbers (www.gla.ac.uk/services/humanresources/harassment_policy.htm).

POINTS TO REFLECT ON . . .

- If an incident occurred would you know how to help the victim immediately?
- Do you know what other support would be available?

10 You are not alone

This chapter contains case studies from individuals in various information sectors, sent in by readers of CILIP's *Library + Information Gazette* who responded to my request for accounts of their experiences.

Introduction

Media coverage – in newspapers and magazines, on the TV and on radio – shows that in recent years there has been a significant increase in the amount of vandalism, aggressive behaviour and bullying everywhere, including in information centres and libraries. Even more worrying is the growth in the number of abusive or violent attacks on members of information and library staff, and the way in which such behaviour affects other information centre and library users.

While it is not the role of staff or employers to solve the underlying problem of violence in our society, it is clear that there is much that individuals and organizations can do to reduce the risk of violence. Judging by the evidence which has accumulated, many library authorities, universities, colleges and organizations are already taking the matter seriously and devising their own preventative measures. Advice, guidance and various procedures which can be adapted to local situations where a problem exists, or is thought to exist, can be found in this book and in other publications listed in the Bibliography in Appendix A. They should also sound a cautionary note to those who do not have an acknowledged problem.

This book is aimed at individual staff members in all types of information centres and libraries, but also at managers, trade unionists, health and safety supervisors, chief officers, elected members and owners, who should all benefit from reading it. If, after reading this book, you believe that you are not properly trained, then you should make sure that you go on a training course so that you are prepared for any acts of aggression, violence or harassment happening to you.

Most people believe that an accident or incident will not happen to them, but the following incidents have really happened to colleagues in the profession here in the UK. They were sent in response to my appeal in CILIP's *Library + Information Gazette* on 15 December 2006.They do not make pleasant reading, but I feel you should be aware of them.

These incidents may be used as a focal point for the setting up of staff discussion groups to raise awareness and perhaps to find out whether there are any problems in your particular information centre or library. Not all of these examples offer solutions. Some tell of the consequences, and others of actions taken.

Example 1

I had to leave my last job because my manager was bullying me and the college was unwilling to believe me. I was so pleased to be offered that post, in one of the postgraduate teaching hospitals. It was a lovely job – my ideal post, in fact. Unfortunately the management of the library passed from a clinical director to the administrative director of operations. Within a couple of weeks the new director had assumed direct control of my budget and told me that I would never achieve anything because I was a woman. He spent the next year sending me long e-mails that told me I was unable to trust people, that he could not work with me, etc. In the end I felt physically sick at seeing an e-mail from him in the inbox and had to ask a friend to vet them first. I took advice from a college harassment officer and followed up her suggestion to pursue this with a senior member of staff. Sadly, that senior person told me I was merely whinging, that this was medicine and that I had to accept 'strong management'. In the end I had to leave.

I must be the world's lousiest medical librarian because I've ended up in another hospital library where my manager, the librarian, is systematically undermining everything that I do. I am excluded from every part of the library's work – work that I could and should be doing is being given to her daughter who she employs specially for the purpose. I am supposed to be delivering information skills training but my role is limited to pressing the enter key to run PowerPoint presentations for the librarian, who leads all training courses. I don't have a role in the library and given that I am on Band 6 I am an expensive resource! I am being given tasks that are uneconomic and unsustainable. Projects that I have attempted to initiate have grounded because the librarian will not work with me. Her aggressive attitude and constant put-downs are impossibly difficult to manage. I went to Occupational Health for advice and was told that although I had sufficient grounds for a complaint, I should not rock the boat by putting in a grievance.

I can't tell you how many times I come home in the evening in tears. I keep getting outbreaks of dermatitis on my hands and legs that I never had before in my life, and I have never had so many migraines as I have had in the last two years.

It feels humiliating to say that, at the age of 43, I am being bullied. I don't really think I'm that incompetent and I'm not an aggressive person. Every hospital I've worked in has all sorts of 'dignity at work' and harassment policies, but seems unable to come to the rescue of staff who find themselves working for a poor manager. I'm not entirely sure what the answer is.

Example 2

I work as a library assistant in a well known university library service, and a few years ago one of my colleagues was promoted to supervisor level. This went to her head and resulted in few folk in the office really liking her, we even have a nickname for her. What she has done to me is rota me for opening duty on the Monday morning on my return from holiday or sickness on a regular basis. We work flexitime so do not have to be in till 9.30.

Last summer I was placed on rota for five consecutive Monday morning openings during the summer vacation. When I pointed this out I was told that people were on training courses, but there was no mention of this in the e-diary. She makes sarcastic comments in the office that everyone can hear, and wages 'hate campaigns' against staff she takes a dislike to.

There is also the issue of student aggression. Two summers ago a female student complained that I was rude to her. She gave no other information. I did not remember the incident, so it can't have been extraordinary. When a more senior supervisor contacted her for more information, she replied that I was not fit to work on a public desk and should be sacked. I have been argued with over fines (what a surprise) and even sworn at on more than one occasion.

Example 3

I worked in an academic library in a postgraduate university until recently. I had worked there for four years. The first three years went well, but as soon as I was promoted, moved away from the issue desk and took on a few more responsibilities, one of my work colleagues turned into the bitch from hell. She never threatened me and wasn't verbally or physically abusive but she criticised, belittled, scorned and excluded me constantly for an entire year. She even started a whispering campaign with other colleagues.

During the summer I'd had enough, so I went, together with another colleague who had been at the end of the bully's poisonous tongue for many more years than I had, to the university librarian (our own manager, although supportive, could not manage the bully, and has since admitted she is scared of her). The university librarian involved Employee Relations, who carried out an 'investigation'.

It was found that my colleague and I were as much to blame, and all three of us were threatened with disciplinary proceedings. I was devastated. I could not understand how they could interview four people who stated what a misery the bully had made their lives, and then say there wasn't 'enough evidence'. My colleague and I weren't allowed to know the nature of the counter-allegations made against us, or who had made them. In the letter giving the results of the investigation they referred to incidents in the past when I hadn't even been working there.

The whole thing was a disaster and we suspect the university just didn't want to rock the boat. The bully had worked there for years and years, was respected and liked by many other people and belonged to the union.

As a result of all the stress I had been under during that year, I started to experience odd physical sensations. I would go extremely pale and start to hyperventilate. My body would feel so heavy I could hardly move and then I would feel tearful. My face would go numb and tingly. I couldn't sleep, either. I went to the doctors thinking, on top of everything else, I'd developed a brain tumour! He diagnosed panic/anxiety attacks and depression, and I'm still being treated for the latter.

The only way I could keep my sanity was to leave, so I started to apply for jobs and would spend hours filling in application forms. I didn't give up until I got one, and I started in my new role two weeks ago. It is maternity leave only, and a side-step away from librarianship. I am now questioning whether to go back into librarianship after my 'breathing space' role is completed. It is ironic that just two days after leaving the university, I received a letter from CILIP telling me my recent application for chartership had been accepted. A bitter-sweet success.

So what lessons have I learned? I've learned that the bully always wins, and that the 'system' works to protect the bully no matter how much it says it advocates the principles of diversity. I have learned never to go down the 'correct' routes. A gun would have been the preferable option, in hindsight, and would have been a lot less messy!!

I have left where I worked and so would not be able to give any helpful tips on how to cope with a bully if I were ever in that situation again. Please excuse the cynicism and bitterness – it is all still a bit raw.

Example 4

I had a horrible experience working in a charity's information service during 2005. Essentially the information service manager was very ill with 'depression' (that is how the condition was referred to, but I think it was more like bipolar disorder) resulting in very poor attendance and performance. As the second in command and only other qualified librarian I had to cover as best I could. That part I could handle.

However, when the manager was at work she was, basically, a bully. I was constantly belittled (including in front of other members of staff), had work taken away from me (even when users made it clear they wanted me to do the work because they knew they would get better results) and was not given any autonomy (even though I was running things single-handedly a lot of the time), etc.

The information service manager's manager soon realized there was a problem and we had a few meetings, first without and then with the information service manager. HR was also involved. But nothing happened and nothing changed. It got to the stage where I was in tears most days and ended up on mild antidepressants. The only thing that stopped me from walking out was fear of never getting another job again. At one stage I thought that they were so frightened of ending up in a tribunal because of not being sympathetic enough to the information service manager that they didn't really care about how it was affecting me or the service.

I did ask HR about grievance procedures but was told that it was just the same as what was happening with regard to the senior manager being involved. I am now given to understand that if I had raised a formal written grievance I could have taken them to a tribunal because they failed to do anything about the bullying.

I started looking for another job after three months there and, after being told I was the second choice for two jobs, nine months later I was offered my current post. I went to my exit interview armed with specific, quantitative, verifiable examples of the information service manager's incompetence and talked about how it affected the service provided and the impact that was having on core business objectives. I kept in touch with a couple of people and was interested to hear that soon after I left the manager was demoted into my old job and a new manager was appointed.

It seems a long time ago now and I'm so happy in my current job that it is hard to remember how bad it was. I'm still working on getting my confidence back though. I find myself checking in with my manager about things that he is happy for me just to get on with, and I'm nervous of piping up with new ideas or opinions in case I get 'shot down' for it.

Example 5

Alas, although you say 'you are not alone' unfortunately the harrassed ones (mainly women) are – because their jobs are on the line if they make a formal complaint (especially in situations where the harrassment is covert). Bullying in the old academic sector is class-ridden (much more than in new universities) and library assistants are treated like handmaids – it is a case of train and groom them to abuse other people (nothing new here). Bullying is mainly performed by women, but men also abuse their power.

I 'escaped' being bullied by women, but from day one the library secretary warned me against the library lech (a permanent member of staff who is still there) and I could not escape, alas, from having him press himself against my back when needing to access a room behind where I was sitting (because in the charming library system library assistants had to do a stint at the porter's desk). The lech only hit on library assistants (which was common knowledge). It's not an awful problem – but an anecdote of how low down the pecking order we are when we start off in a library.

Example 6

Aggression occurred in a small academic library (three employees). The aggressor was the library assistant (LA), the most junior of the three, and aggression occurred for the duration of her employment. To a large extent, it was merely a matter of rudeness: of not answering when she was spoken to; of combing her hair directly in front of others; of not saying 'excuse me' when she opened a drawer directly in front of others – nothing in itself major, but creating an unpleasant atmosphere.

Stress arose because of the low quantity and quality of the LA's work. She was slow, inaccurate and unwilling, for example doing as little shelving as she could possibly get away with, and ignoring her jobs of answering the telephone and greeting people when they came into the library (she kept her head down to force others to substitute for her). By being stroppy, she was skilful at evading work.

The Assistant Librarian described her as difficult and as barely up to her job; however, she was reluctant to say anything directly to the LA for fear of the retaliation being a formal accusation of bullying. We resorted to subterfuge: one of the instructions concerning the LA was to delete all her catalogue records as she did them, in view of their low quality, but to do this without letting the LA know of it, as she would resent correction.

I ended up doing much of the LA's work in addition to mine. Having a great deal of junior work forced upon me induced stress, which was not immediately decreased by the Fellow Librarian's comments that although employing the LA had been a mistake, we could not get rid of her, that it would not be fair to expect the standard of work from her that one would from an Oxbridge graduate, and that it was important to know what people of low ability were like. The LA's incompetence was the major factor that led to me having a breakdown and being signed off work for three weeks. I contracted flu immediately after that, and was away for another week. The major single example of the LA's bullying was to complain about me collapsing at work. I had applied for, and received, a day's annual leave, being too unwell to work (actually an irregular proceeding, as when one is sick one is supposed to take sick leave, not annual leave, but I did not realize this at the time, merely trying to avoid further sick leave after a month-long certified absence). The LA complained and had it revoked.

After just over ten months, the LA left, rendering the library a happier place, and she subsequently moved out of library work. I left as soon as I gained my library qualification. When I went, I received a thank you letter from the library committee for all the work I had done. It was apparently the first time that a member of staff had received a thank you letter, and may at least partly have been an indirect way of acknowledging the unpleasantness endured from the LA. After I broke down, the college paid two-thirds of the cost of counselling for several months.

Looking back, I think that the LA felt insecure: I was informed later that she had suffered from jealousy. We learned later that she had applied unsuccessfully to Oxbridge. As her school had sufficient experience of Oxbridge applicants to know that she could not possibly succeed, this betokened pushy parents. At the college, she was the only 'failure' among people who either already had an Oxbridge degree, or were working towards one. Nobody regarded her English degree from a cathedral town university, about which she boasted continually, as a particular achievement, or, indeed, thought at all about her background. Also, in an atmosphere of general competence, a spotlight was inevitably shone on her slowness and incompetence, which cannot have been easy.

Experiencing the LA was extremely unpleasant and, six years later, the scars have not disappeared. Moreover, one's confidence is shaken and one mistrusts oneself after such an experience (here I was reinforced by the assurance of librarians from a couple of other institutions who said that we could have dismissed her for inability to do her work). Yet it is also possible to learn positively from the experience. The LA's predecessor had been very good, and I had taken the predecessor's good work for granted; experience of the LA rendered me far more appreciative of good work subsequently. Being bullied gave me resilience, and counselling helped to give me a sense of perspective about the position of one's remunerated employment in one's life. The jealousy, albeit nasty, also helped: awareness of somebody else wanting gifts sharpened my sense of obligation to others to use what gifts one has for the good of the profession.

Example 7

I have witnessed incidents of bullying while working in two libraries. While working as a librarian for a government library in 1996 I worked for a senior librarian who picked on a newly recruited assistant librarian (ALib). This took the form of telling her it would be necessary for her to become involved in a particular library committee if she wanted to succeed in the post.

The ALib was very nervous and intimidated, and became so worried about her performance that she sometimes used to work until 9 p.m. in the evenings. I explained to the senior librarian that I felt he should intervene and explain that she need not work such long hours, but he refused. I finally told the HR manager, who approached his manager about the issue.

From then on I felt the situation was dealt with very well as his manager (not a librarian but a Grade 7) talked to me and I was able to explain my concerns. The Grade 7 told the senior librarian to stop picking on her and matters improved. I left shortly after this but subsequently heard that the ALIb resigned and claimed constructive dismissal.

At the time there were three other professional librarians (me included) and he didn't pick on us in the same way.

From 2000 to 2006 I worked in a City law firm and witnessed two of my colleagues being bullied over a four-and-a-half year period by our manager. This took the form of publicly telling them off and making snide remarks to them. Both were in a financial situation where they could not afford to stop working, and I felt the manager played on this. One colleague had a temporary work permit and had found the post via an agency that helped people on benefits secure work. The other was an older man who was past retirement age. His continued service was dependent on the manager's agreement. During this period I made five complaints to HR about her, but was never supported. I was told that HR could only intervene if I made a formal complaint or if I and my colleagues made a joint complaint. This felt very difficult as the two colleagues who were being bullied were so frightened of her. She also treated another colleague with very little respect and the situation became so bad that he was moved to another department.

In September 2005 a new temporary member of staff arrived and the manager started to bully her too. Our new colleague immediately reported her to HR and made a formal complaint of bullying. The situation was finally resolved in March 2006 when the manager resigned. The remaining staff divided into two camps: those who supported her and those who did not. What was very interesting was that the two people who had been bullied rallied round and were reluctant to say how she had treated them (at the time of the complaint we were all interviewed by HR) and have subsequently become on friendly terms with her. From what I have read about bullying, though, I believe it is not that uncommon that 'victims' befriend their persecutors.

I feel strongly that bullying is a very serious issue which causes a lot of distress for those concerned. However, personally I would think twice about standing up for my colleagues in view of what happened in my last post.

I have now returned to work in the public sector and feel confident that if I did witness any bullying again it would be dealt with appropriately. I have been able to join a union again and my employer has a 'fairness at work' policy so, for me, this feels safer.

Example 8

I think that your book will be invaluable in helping people realize that they are not the only ones suffering, and that it is generally not their fault. In my case, someone tried to make me feel that his verbal abuse resulted from, and indeed was justified by, my incompetence. (Since then, two employers have offered me a renewal of a contract, or a permanent post after months in a temporary post, so they chose to employ me knowing what my work was like.)

The shouting and verbal abuse, invariably in front of my staff, was in many ways easier to tolerate, as the staff all knew what he was like (I was by no means the only sufferer), and they were used to ignoring him. What I really found difficult was the more insidious approach, whereby he often 'moved the goalposts', so that whatever I did was wrong. Even though I'd done what I had been asked to do, I would be deemed to have failed because I hadn't done something else. Setting unrealistic targets was also common – I got into trouble for not supervising my staff closely enough while I was on holiday, for example, or because my department got through less work than usual when staff were absent through sickness or holidays.

At the time, I read up on office bullying and dealing with difficult people, and learned about being assertive and transactional analysis. It was great to discover that there were things I could try. But none of it seemed to have any effect. Then someone pointed out that the techniques normally recommended in self-help books will only work when the person you are dealing with is within a certain range of 'normal': maybe at the extreme end of the range, but more or less normal. Some people are beyond that range, and so the techniques will not work with them. When that happens, I believe that you have to accept that you cannot change that sort of person's behaviour. You either accept that it happens and just cope with it, or you get out. I decided not to settle for just coping with it, thereby writing off the rest of my career, so I resigned, and was lucky enough to be offered another job a few days later. Many years later, the bullying behaviour is still going on, I hear.

Example 9

While I cannot, and will not, discuss any details of instances of violence, aggression, etc. which may have occurred while I was head of library services – which I am sure you will understand – I will offer the following scenarios.

Managing conflict between staff

Two library assistants are best mates, go on holiday together and return refusing to talk to each other. Before you know where you are life is disrupted as two people refuse to communicate with each other and, worse still, refuse to do counter duties together (and if you try to ignore the situation and insist that they are timetabled together, there is not a library user left who does not know that your staff are at war). Since I have been in and out of other libraries and museums I have been astounded at how common this problem appears to be, and how bad as managers we seem to be at conflict resolution.

Measuring stress levels in staff

Going in and out of organizations is fascinating when you see the contrast between what a line manager thinks staff are doing/coping with, and what the staff think that line manager knows! Do managers often measure the stress levels of their staff? Do managers know that most health and safety managers/officers and HR departments are able to do this?

Managing perception against reality

My belief is that this is one of the biggest issues when talking about unpacking aggression in the workplace. The argument from library assistants goes something like this: 'There is no point in calling for security, they will take hours to get here, I might as well have a go at sorting out this group of youths myself.' Showing staff a CCTV recording with the timer on full view, so that they can clearly see the number of minutes that pass between pressing a call button and security appearing, is sometimes a start. But digging people out of the pit of 'there's no point' is a long hard process – one, however, that must be won if the manager wants to tackle aggression from users.

When is firmness interpreted as aggression and when is aggression bullying?

I have sometimes been told that I chair meetings very aggressively. In other situations I have been told that my chairing is not firm enough! I have often read definitions of bullying, and many are very useful. However, I often feel that the point should be made that this is a subjective area that has as much to do with relationships and context as a list of items to be ticked off.

Example 10

Working in a successful engineering consultancy was the background to a change of happiness for a librarian who had been enjoying her work until the arrival of a new member of staff. The new person deliberately tried to undermine the librarian's confidence at every opportunity for six months. She writes:

The individual incidents sound completely pathetic but it has made my life miserable . . . I've felt ill just being in the same office as her. I confess (the coward in me) I'm terrified of what she has been doing but she has taken it too far – now that she has started on others in her new role as personnel officer. She has introduced a new sickness form to be signed when we have time off: something we've never had before and never really needed. One of my colleagues asked her why she'd introduced it. She said: 'Because I can'. I just feel outraged by her behaviour. I think she's getting all too carried away with her new role and feels very powerful.

She's definitely targeting those of the support staff that she feels threatened by (in the most spiteful way) to bring us into line and under her control. Well, the gloves are off. I've had enough and I'm very grateful to the likes of you and the other professional contacts for restoring a bit of confidence in myself.

I've decided I'm going to make an official complaint next week when I have my meeting with our managing director (who is my line manager). I've just had enough of it so I'm going to type up a note outlining all the incidents.

Sadly the outcome of this was that MD did listen but did not want to take any action! So the librarian is now looking for another job.

Example 11

'You are going to need courage, honesty and openness with people. You are going to need to break out of your comfort zone. That first day in a new job or the first month doing something new is always difficult, wondering if you have done the right thing. You are going to have to be prepared for envy and jealousy because your fellow professionals and other colleagues can get very jealous if you are the sort of person who wants to do things differently, or get on quickly, or break the mould slightly. Be prepared for bullying. When I returned from a secondment, my manager and the person who had had a temporary promotion in the job that I had left didn't expect me back, so I went through a really unpleasant time. I didn't realize it myself, but a senior manager pointed out that they were very subtly bullying me. Thankfully she helped me to deal with it.'

Conclusion

These case studies demonstrate not only how people can suffer in the workplace but also how victimization can result in devastating and long-term effects. Hopefully the knowledge, advice, guidance and, very importantly, the pieces of legislation that have been made available in the last few years will offer some support and hope to anyone who thinks they are alone.

The cases also demonstrate that a weak management can allow staff to suffer – generally because managers are not trained sufficiently in mediation and conflict resolution skills. Anyone who is entrusted with management must be able to grasp the nettle and act to resolve problems that are happening around them. *No one* should have to suffer at work!

Appendices

Appendix A
Bibliography

Arranged alphabetically by author, these publications will give you further information and offer ideas for training and training courses. In the past ten years or so, a wealth of publications have been produced to help people cope with all forms of aggression and conflict in different work sectors.

In addition, you can arrange a 15-day free-of-charge trial of the OSH UPDATE service (www.oshupdate.com), which contains thousands of references on all aspects of aggression and conflict, many with links to full text guidance and advice. Go to the website to register your interest in a trial.

ACAS (2006) *Managing Attendance and Employee Turnover*, www.acas.org.uk/index.aspx?articleid=1183.

ACAS (2007) *Bullying and Harassment at Work: a guide for managers and employers*, www.acas.org.uk/index.aspx?articleid=794.

ACAS (2007) *Bullying and Harassment at Work: guidance for employees*, www.acas.org.uk/index.aspx?articleid=515&detailid=537.

Adams, A. and Crawford, N. (1992) *Bullying at Work: how to confront and overcome it*, Virago Press.

Amati, C. A. and Scaife, R. (2006) *Investigation of the Links Between Psychological Ill-health, Stress and Safety*, HSE Research Report RR 488, Keil Centre and Health and Safety Executive, www.hse.gov.uk/research/rrhtm/rr488.htm.

Andersson, L. and Pearson, C. (1999) Tit for Tat? The spiralling effect of incivility in the workplace, *Academy of Management Review,* **24** (3), 452–71.

Arnold, J., Cooper, C. L. and Robertson, I. T. (1998) *Work Psychology: understanding human behaviour in the workplace*, 3rd edn, Pearson Education Ltd.

Baron, R. and Neuman, J. (1996) Workplace Violence and Workplace Aggression: evidence on their relative frequency and potential causes, *Aggressive Behaviour*, **22**, 161–73.

Baron, R. and Neuman, J. (1998) Workplace Aggression – the Iceberg Beneath the Tip of Workplace Violence: evidence on its forms, frequency and targets, *Public Administration Quarterly*, **21**, 446–64.

Björkqvist, K., Österman, K. and Hjelt-Bäck, M. (1994) Aggression Among University Employees, *Aggressive Behavior*, **20**, 173–84.

Brady, C. (1999) Surviving the Incident. In Leather, P., Brady, C., Lawrence, C., Beale, D. and Cox, T. (eds), *Work-related Violence: assessment and intervention,* Routledge.

Braverman, M. (1999) *Preventing Workplace Violence*, Sage Publications.

Burke, R. J. and Richardsen, A. M. (2000) Organizational-level Interventions Designed to Reduce Occupational Stressors. In Dewe, P., Leiter, M. and Cox, T. (eds), *Coping, Health and Organizations*, Taylor and Francis.

Cardy, C. and Lamplugh, D. (1994) *Training for Personal Safety at Work*, Gower.

Cartwright, S. and Cooper, C. L. (1997) *Managing Workplace Stress*, Sage Publications Inc.

Chappell, D. and Di Martino, V. (2006) *Violence at Work*, 3rd edn, International Labour Organization.

Chartered Institute of Personnel and Development (2006a) *Bullying at Work: beyond policies to a culture of respect*, CIPD, www.cipd.co.uk/subjects/dvsequl/harassmt/bullyatwork0405.htm.

Chartered Institute of Personnel and Development (2006b) Nowhere to Go: bullying at work, *People Management*, 6 December.

Chartered Management Institute (2005) *Bullying at Work: the experience of managers*, executive summary and guidelines for managers on tackling bullying are available from www.managers.org/bullying.

Collier, R. (1995) *Combating Sexual Harassment in the Workplace*, Open University.

Confederation of British Industry (2000) *Focus on Absence: absence and labour turnover survey 2000*, CBI.

Confederation of British Industry (2007) News Release: workplace absence costs UK £12.2bn – new survey, www.cbi.org.uk.

Cooper, C. L. and Cartwright, S. (1997) An Intervention Strategy for Workplace Stress, *Journal of Psychosomatic Research*, **43**, 7–16.

Cooper, C. L. and Jackson, S. (1997) *Creating Tomorrow's Organizations: a handbook for future research in organizational behavior*, Wiley.

Cooper, C. L., Liukkonen, P. and Cartwright, S. (1996) *Stress Prevention in the Workplace: assessing the costs and benefits for organizations*, European Foundation for the Improvement of Living and Working Conditions.

Cooper, C. L. and Marshall, J. (1976) Occupational Sources of Stress: a review of the literature relating to coronary heart disease and mental ill health, *Journal of Occupational Psychology*, **49**, 11–28.

Cooper, C. and Robertson, I. (2001) *Well-being in Organisations: a reader for students and practitioners*, Wiley.

Craig, M. and Phillips, E. (1991) *Office Workers' Survival Handbook: a guide to fighting health hazards in the office*, Women's Press.

Cox, T. (1978) *Stress*, Macmillan.

Cox, T. (1993) *Stress Research and Stress Management: putting theory to work*, HSE Contract Research Report 61, www.hse.gov.uk/research/crr_htm/1993/orr93061.htm.

Cox, T. and Cox, S. (1993) *Psychosocial and Organizational Hazards: monitoring and control*, Occasional Series in Occupational Health No. 5, World Health Organization (Europe).

Cox, T. and Griffiths, A. (2006) Defining a Case of Work-related Stress, HSE Research Report RR 449, HSE, www.hse.gov.uk/research/rrhtm/rr449.htm.

Cox, T., Griffith, A. and Rial-Gonzalez, E. (2000) *Research on Work-related stress*, European Agency for Safety and Health at Work.

Cox, T. and Leather, P. (1994) The Prevention of Violence at Work: application of a cognitive behavioural theory. In Cooper, C. L. and Robertson, I. T. (eds), *International Review of Industrial and Organizational Psychology 1994*, Wiley.

Daniels, K. and Harris, C. (2000) Work, Psychological Well-being and

Performance, *Occupational Medicine – Oxford,* **50**, 304–9.

Di Martino, V. (1992) Occupational Stress: a preventive approach. In *ILO Conditions of Work Digest, 11/2,* International Labour Office, 3–21.

Di Martino, V. and Pujol, J. (2000) *The Safe Work Training Package on Drugs and Alcohol, Violence, Stress, Tobacco and HIV/AIDS,* International Labour Organization Working Paper.

Dorman, P. (2000) *The Economics of Safety, Health and Well-being at Work: an overview,* International Labour Organization.

Einarsen, S., Hoel, H., Zapf, D. and Cooper, C. (2003) *Bullying and Emotional Abuse in the Workplace,* Taylor and Francis.

European Foundation for the Improvement of Living and Working Conditions (1994) *European Conference on Stress at Work – A Call for Action: proceedings, Brussels, 9–10 November 2003,* Mossink, J. C. and De Gier, H. G. (eds).

European Foundation for the Improvement of Living and Working Conditions (1996) *Assessing Working Conditions: the European practice.*

European Foundation for the Improvement of Living and Working Conditions (1997) *Second European Survey on Working Conditions.*

European Foundation for the Improvement of Living and Working Conditions (2000) *Third European Survey on Working Conditions.*

European Trade Union Technical Bureau for Health and Safety (2002) Stress at Work, *TUTB Newsletter,* Special Issue No. 19–20, September, http://hesa.etui-rehs.org/uk/newsletter/files/Newsletter-20.pdf.

Flannery, R. B. (1996) Violence in the Workplace, 1970–1995: a review of the literature, *Aggression and Violent Behavior,* **1**, 57–68.

Gordon, F. and Risley, D. (1999) *The Costs to Britain of Workplace Accidents and Work-related Ill Health in 1995/6,* 2nd edn, HSE Books.

Gutek, B. A. and Koss, M. P. (1993) Changed Women and Changed Organisations: consequences of and coping with sexual harassment, *Journal of Vocational Behaviour,* **42**, 28–48.

Hazards (1994) Bullying at Work, *Hazards,* **48** (2), Autumn.

Health and Safety Authority, Ireland (1995) *Violence at Work.*

Health and Safety Authority, Ireland (2002) *Code of Practice in the Prevention of Workplace Bullying,* www.hsa.ie/publisher/storefront/product_detail.jsp?_dir_itemID_53.

Health and Safety Executive (1993) *Prevention of Violence to Staff in Banks and Building Societies*, HS(G) 100, HSE Books.

Health and Safety Executive (1995a) *Preventing Violence to Staff*, HS(G) 133, HSE Books.

Health and Safety Executive (1995b) *Stress at Work: a guide for employers*, HS(G) 116, HSE Books.

Health and Safety Executive (1997) *Violence to Staff*, IND(G) 69L, HSE Books.

Health and Safety Executive (2004) *Management Standards for Tackling Work-related Stress*, including *Short Guide to the Management Standards* and *Overview of the Management Standards Approach*, www.hse.gov.uk/stress/standards/index.htm.

Health and Safety Executive (2006a) *5 Steps to Risk Assessment*, IND(G) 163L, HSE Books, www.hse.gov.uk/pubns/indg163.pdf.

Health and Safety Executive (2006b) *Bullying at Work: a review of the literature*, Health and Safety Laboratories Report 603, Health and Safety Executive, www.hse.gov.uk/research/hsl_pdf/2006/hs10630.pdf.

Health and Safety Executive (2006c) *Charity and Voluntary Worker: a guide to health and safety at work*, 2nd edn, HSE Books.

Health and Safety Executive (2006d) *The Essentials of Health and Safety at Work*, 4th edn, HSE Books.

Health and Safety Executive (n.d.) Real Solutions, Real People, information pack, ISBN 0-7176-2767-5; for full details see pages 53–4.

Hodson, R., Roscigno, V. J. and Lopez, S. H. (2006) Workplace Bullying in Organizational and Interactional Context, *Work and Occupations*, **33** (4), 382–416.

Hoel, H., Rayner, C. and Cooper, C. L. (1999) Workplace Bullying, *International Review of Industrial and Organizational Psychology*, **14**, 195–230, http://taylorandfrancis.metapress.com/(f5hsezzoi0yqoj55jtgscnvb)/app/home/linking.asp?referrer=linking&target=contribution&id=u0yqe748q3ja4pgp&backto=contribution,1,1;issue,8,16;journal,10,100;linkingpublicationresults,1:104400,1.

Hoel, H., Sparks, K. and Cooper, C. L. (2005) *The Cost of Violence/Stress at Work and the Benefits of a Violence/Stress-free Working Environment*,

University of Manchester Institute of Science and Technology, for
International Labour Office in Geneva,
www.ilo.org/public/english/protection/safework/whpwb/econo/costs.pdf.

Jacobson, B. H., Aldano, S. G., Goetzel, R. Z., Vardell, K. D., Adams, T.
B. and Pietras, R. J. (1996) The Relationship Between Perceived Stress
and Self Reported Illness-Related Absenteeism, *American Journal of
Health Promotion*, **11**, 54–61.

Kivimaki, M., Virtanen, M., Vartia, M., Elovainio, M., Vahtera, J. and
Keltikangas-Jarvinen, L. (2003) Workplace Bullying and the Risk of
Cardiovascular Disease and Depression, *Occupational and Environmental
Medicine*, **60**, 779–83.

Kompier, M. and Cooper, C. L. (1999) *Preventing Stress, Improving
Productivity: European case studies in the workplace*, Routledge.

Kompier, M., Cooper, C. L. and Geurts, S. (2000) A Multiple Case Study
Approach to Work Stress Prevention in Europe, *European Journal of
Work and Organizational Psychology*, **9**, 371–400.

Lau, V. C. S., Au, W. T. and Ho, J. M. C. (2003) A Qualitative and
Quantitative Review of Antecedents of Counterproductive Behaviour in
Organizations, *Journal of Business and Psychology*, **18** (1), 73–99.

Leather, P., Brady, C., Lawrence, C., Beale, D. and Cox, T. (1999) *Work-
related Violence: assessment and intervention*, Routledge.

Leather, P., Lawrence, C., Beale, D., Cox, T. and Dixon, R. (1998)
Exposure to Occupational Violence and the Buffering Effects of Intra-
organizational Support, *Work and Stress*, **12**, 161–78.

Levi, L. and Lunde-Jensen, P. (1995) *A Model for Assessing the Costs of
Stressors at National Level: socio-economic costs of stress in two EU member
states*, European Foundation for the Improvement of Living and
Working Conditions.

Leymann, H. (1996) The Content and Development of Mobbing at Work,
European Journal of Work and Organizational Psychology, **5** (2), 165–84.

Leymann, H. and Gustafsson, A. (1996) Mobbing at Work and the
Development of Post-traumatic Stress Disorders, *European Journal of
Work and Organizational Psychology*, **5**, 251–75.

Library Association (1987) *Violence in Libraries: preventing aggressive and
unacceptable behaviour in libraries*, pamphlet (no longer available).

Lindsay, P. (2006) *Violence and Aggression in the Workplace: a practical guide for all healthcare staff*, Radcliffe.

Mikkelsen, E. G. and Einarsen, S. (2002) Basic Assumptions and Symptoms of Post-traumatic Stress Among Victims of Bullying at Work, *European Journal of Work and Organizational Psychology*, **11** (1), 87–111.

Mikkelsen, E. G. and Einarsen, S. (2002) Relationships Between Exposure to Bullying at Work and Psychological and Psychosomatic Health Complaints: the role of state negative affectivity and generalised self efficacy, *Scandinavian Journal of Psychology*, **43**, 397–405.

MSF (1995) *Bullying at Work: how to tackle it. A guide for MSF representatives and members*, MSF Health and Safety Office.

Murphy, L. R. and Cooper, C. L. (2000) *Healthy and Productive Work: an international perspective*, Taylor and Francis.

Notelaers, G., De Witte, H. and Einarsen, S. (2003) Organisational Antecedents of Bullying at the Workplace. In Giga, S., Flaxman, P., Houdmont, J. and Ertel, M. (eds), *Occupational Health Psychology: flexibility, quality of working life and health. Proceedings from the 5th European Academy of Occupational Health Psychology conference, November 2003.*

O'Moore, M., Seyne, E., McGuire, C. and Smith, M. (1998) Victims of Bullying at Work in Ireland, *Journal of Occupational Health and Safety – Australia/New Zealand*, **14** (6), 569–74.

Overell, S. (1995) Union Demands Action to Stop Bullying at Work, *People Management*, 21 September, 10.

Overell, S. (1995) HSE Tightens its Line on Violence in the Workplace, *People Management*, 5 October, 8–9.

Peck, S. (2006) *Stress at Work,* Labour Research Department Publications.

Poyner, B. (1988) The Prevention of Violence to Staff, *Journal of Health and Safety*, **1**, (July), 19–26.

Poyner, B. (1989) Working Against Violence, *Occupational Health*, **41** (8), 209–11.

Poyner, B. and Warne, C. for the Health and Safety Executive and Tavistock Institute of Human Relations (1986) *Violence to Staff: a basis for assessment and prevention*, HSE Books.

Poyner, B. and Warne, C. for the Health and Safety Executive and Tavistock Institute of Human Relations (1988) *Preventing Violence to*

Staff, HSE Books.

Price Spratlen, L. (1995) Interpersonal Conflict which Includes Mistreatment in a University Workplace, *Violence and Victims*, **10**, 285–97.

Quine, L. (1999) Workplace Bullying in NHS Community Trust: staff questionnaire survey, *British Medical Journal*, **318**, 228–32.

Quinlan, M. (1999) The Implications of Labour Market Restructuring in Industrial Societies for Occupational Health and Safety, *Economic and Industrial Democracy*, **20**, 427–60.

Randall, T. (1990) Domestic Violence Intervention Calls for More than Treating Injuries, *Journal of the American Medical Association*, **264**, 939–40.

Rayner, C. and Hoel, H. (1997) A Summary Review of Literature Relating to Workplace Bullying, *Journal of Community and Applied Psychology*, **7**, 181–91.

Rayner, C., Hoel, H. and Cooper, C. L. (2002) *Workplace Bullying: what we know, who is to blame and what can we do?*, Taylor and Francis.

Reich, R. B. and Dear, J. A. (1996) Guidelines for Preventing Workplace Violence for Health Care and Social Service Workers. In VandenBos, G. R. and Bulatao, E. Q. (eds), *Violence on the Job*, American Psychological Association.

Reynolds, P. (1994) *Dealing with Crime and Aggression at Work: a handbook for organizational action*, McGraw-Hill.

Rick, J., Thomson, L., Briner, R. B., O'Regan, S. and Daniels, K. (2002) *Review of Existing Supporting Scientific Knowledge to Underpin Standards of Good Practice for Key Work-related Stressors – Phase 1*, HSE Research Report RR024, www.hse.gov.uk/research/rrhtm/rr024.htm.

Rogers, K. and Kelloway, E. K. (1997) Violence at Work: personal and organizational outcomes, *Journal of Occupational Health Psychology*, **2**, 63–71.

Royal Society for the Prevention of Accidents (n.d.) *Work Stress: advice on its prevention and management*, www.rospa.co.uk/stress/conflict/index.htm.

Royal Society for the Prevention of Accidents (n.d.) *Work Stress: a brief guide for line managers*, www.rospa.co.uk/stress/conflict/index.htm.

Runyan, C. W., Zakocs, R. C. and Zwerling, C. (2000) Administrative and Behavioral Interventions for Workplace Violence Prevention, *American*

Journal of Preventive Medicine, **18**, 116–27.

Sauter, S., Murphy, L. R. and Hurrell, J. J. (1990) A National Strategy for the Prevention of Work-related Psychological Disorders, *American Psychologist*, **45**, 1146–58.

Schneider, K. T., Swan, S. and Fitzgerald, L. F. (1997) Job-related and Psychological Effects of Sexual Harassment in the Workplace: empirical evidence from two organizations, *Journal of Applied Psychology*, **82**, 401–14.

Scott, A. (2007) The De-stress Call, *People Management*, **25** (January), 16–17.

Smith, A. (2000) The Scale of Perceived Occupational Stress, *Occupational Medicine*, **50**, 294–8.

Spiers, C. (2003) *Tolley's Managing Stress in the Workplace*, LexisNexis UK.

Standing, H. and Nicolini, D. (1997) *Review of Workplace Related Violence*, HMSO.

Stranks, J. (2005) *Stress at Work: management and prevention*, Butterworth-Heinemann.

Stranks J. (2006) *Health and Safety Pocket Book*, Butterworth-Heinemann.

Sutherland, V. J. and Cooper, C. L. (2000) *Strategic Stress Management: an organizational approach*, Macmillan Press Ltd.

www.suzylamplugh.org/products/g08.sthml.

The Suzy Lamplugh Trust (1995) *Beating Aggression*, Suzy Lamplugh Trust.

The Suzy Lamplugh Trust (1995) *The Pocket Fast Guide to Personal Safety at Work*, Suzy Lamplugh Trust/Hascombe Enterprises Ltd.

The Suzy Lamplugh Trust (2007) *First Steps to Stress Management at Work*, DVD, www.suzylamplugh.org/store/videos.shtml.

The Suzy Lamplugh Trust (2007) *Living Safely*, Taylor, S. (1998) *Employee Resourcing*, Institute of Personnel and Development.

Tehrani, N. (2003) Counselling and Rehabilitating Employees Involved with Bullying. In Einarsen, S., Hoel, S., Zapf, D. and Cooper, C. (eds) *Bullying and Emotional Abuse in the Workplace*, Taylor and Francis.

Trades Union Congress (1988) Violence to Staff: report on recent work, *Trades Union Congress Health and Safety Bulletin*, **8**, 9–11.

Trades Union Congress (2006) *Focus on Health and Safety*, www.tuc.org.uk/h_and_s/tuc-12679-f0.cfm.

TUTB Newsletter (2002) Special Issue: Stress at Work, **19–20**,

(September), European Trade Union Technical Bureau for Health and Safety, http://hesa.etui-rehs.org/uk/newsletter/files/newsletter-20.pdf.

Universities and Colleges Employers Association (2006) *Preventing and Tackling Stress at Work: an approach for higher education.*

US National Institute for Occupational Safety and Health (2006) *Workplace Violence Prevention Strategies and Research Needs: report from the Conference Partnering in Workplace Violence Prevention: Translating Research to Practice, 17–19 November 2004, Baltimore, Maryland*, Publication No. 2006–144, Centers for Disease Control and Prevention, www.cdc.gov/niosh.

Vartia, M. (1996) The Sources of Bullying: psychological work environment and organizational climate, *European Journal of Work and Organizational Psychology*, **5**, 203–14.

Vartia, M. (2001) Consequences of Workplace Bullying with Respect to the Well-being of its Targets and the Observers of Bullying, *Scandinavian Journal of Work Environment and Health*, **27** (1), 63–9.

Vartia, M., Korppoo, L., Fallenius, S. and Mattila, M. (2003) Workplace Bullying: the role of occupational health services. In Einarsen, S., Hoel, H., Zapf, D. ad Cooper, C. (eds), *Bullying and Emotional Abuse in the Workplace*, Taylor and Francis.

Voss, M., Floderus, B. and Diderichsen, F. (2001) Physical, Psychosocial and Organizational Factors Relative to Sickness Absence: a study based on Sweden Post, *Occupational Environmental Medicine*, **58**, 178–84.

Warshaw, L. J. and Messite, J. (1996) Workplace Violence: preventive and interventive strategies, *Journal of Occupational and Environmental Medicine*, **38**, 993–1006.

Wynne, R., Clarkin, N., Cox, T. and Griffiths, A. (1997) *Guidance on the Prevention of Violence at Work*, Ref. CE/VI-4/97, European Commission.

Zapf, D., Knorz, C. and Kulla, M. (1996) On the Relationship Between Mobbing Factors and Job Content, Social Work Environment and Health Outcomes, *European Journal of Work and Organizational Psychology*, **5** (2), 215–37.

Zapf, D., Einarsen, S., Hoel, H. and Vartia, M. (2003) Empirical Findings on Bullying in the Workplace. In Einarsen, S., Hoel, H., Zapf, D. and Cooper, C., *Bullying and Emotional Abuse in the Workplace*, Taylor and Francis.

Appendix B
Websites

Many of these websites contain links to other resources and organizations.

ACAS
    www.acas.org.uk
Amicus
    www.amicustheunion.org
Andrea Adams Trust
    www.andreaadamstrust.org
Association of Personal Injury Lawyers
    www.apil.com
Bullying Online
    www.bullyonline.org/index.htm
Carole Spiers Group
    www.carolespiersgroup.com
Chartered Institution of Personnel and Development
    www.cipd.co.uk/research
    www.cipd.co.uk/subjects/dvsequl/harassmt/harrass.htm?issrchres=1
Health and Safety Authority – Republic of Ireland
    www.hsa.ie
Health and Safety Executive
    www.hse.gov.uk/stress/standards/about.htm.
    www.hse.gov.uk/violence/index.htm
International Stress Management Association UK
    www.isma.org.uk

Royal Society for the Prevention of Accidents (RoSPA)

www.rospa.com

Samaritans

www.samaritans.org

www.stressdownday.org

The Suzy Lamplugh Trust

www.suzylamplugh.org

Trades Union Congress (TUC)

www.tuc.org

US National Institute for Occupational Safety and Health (NIOSH)

www.cdc.gov/niosh/about.html

Workplace Health Connect

www.workplacehealthconnect.co.uk

Appendix C
Advice centres

ACAS

Tel: +44 (0) 8457 474747

www.acas.org.uk

ACAS is the employment relations service for England, Scotland and Wales. It offers practical, independent and impartial advice to employers, employees and their representatives. ACAS encourages people to work together effectively, and aims to promote good practice in the workplace and to help resolve disputes. The website gives details of all the regional ACAS offices, which usually operate Monday–Friday, 08.00–18.00.

(See also their Code of Practice and Grievance Procedure guidelines on pages 88–9.)

Amicus

General Secretary, 35 King Street, London WC2E 8JG, UK

www.amicustheunion.org

The Amicus website takes enquiries and the regional offices, etc. are also listed. Search the site for information on bullying, etc.

Andrea Adams Trust

Hova House, 1 Hova Villas, Hove, East Sussex BN3 3DH, UK

Tel: +44 (0) 1273 704 900

Fax: +44 (0) 1273 704 900

E-mail: mail@andreaadamstrust.org

www.andreaadamstrust.org

The Andrea Adams Trust is the world's only non-political, non-profit-making charity operating as a focus for the diverse and complex problems caused by bullying behaviour in the workplace.

Association of Personal Injury Lawyers

11 Castle Quay, Castle Boulevard, Nottingham NG7 1FW, UK

Tel: +44 (0) 870 609 1958

www.apil.com

The Association has over 2500 members able to give medical and legal advice; they undertake special plaintiff work.

British Association for Counselling and Psychotherapy

BACP House, Unit 15 St John's Business Park, Lutterworth, Leicestershire LE17 4HB, UK

Tel: +44 (0) 870 443 5252

Fax: +44 (0) 870 443 5161

E-mail: bacp@bacp.co.uk

www.bacp.co.uk

The BACP offers guidance and advice.

Chartered Institution of Personnel and Development (CIPD)

151 The Broadway, London SW19 1JQ, UK

Tel: +44 (0) 20 8612 6200

Fax +44 (0) 20 8612 6201

E-mail: www.cipd.co.uk/contactus

www.cipd.co.uk

This professional body for personnel and human resources managers offers guidance and advice on a range of personnel matters.

Chartered Management Institute

3rd Floor, 2 Savoy Court, The Strand, London WC2R 0EZ, UK

Tel: +44 (0) 20 7497 0580

Fax: +44(0) 20 7497 0463

E-mail: enquiries@managers.org.uk

www.managers.org.uk

> The Institute is a professional management body offering guidance and advice.

CILIP: the Chartered Institute of Library and Information Professionals

Information and Advice, 7 Ridgmount Street, London WC1E 7AE, UK

Tel: +44 (0) 20 7255 0500

Fax: +44 (0) 20 7255 0501

E-mail: info@cilip.org.uk

www.cilip.org.uk

> CILIP is a professional body for information and library staff; it offers advice, guidance and training.

Citizens Advice Bureaux

> Check your local telephone directory for a local number.
> CAB offers guidance and advice.

Health and Safety Authority (Republic of Ireland)

The Metropolitan Building, James Joyce Street, Dublin 1, Republic of Ireland

Tel: +353 (0) 1 890 289 389

Fax: +353 (0) 1 614 7020

www.hsa.ie

> The Authority offers health and safety guidance and advice to those suffering workplace aggression and violence.

Health and Safety Executive

Tel: +44 (0) 845 345 0055

www.hse.gov.uk

The HSE offers health and safety guidance and advice to those suffering workplace aggression and violence. It also produces publications.

Health and Safety Executive for Northern Ireland (HSENI)

83 Ladas Drive, Belfast BT6 9FR, Northern Ireland

Tel: +44 (0) 800 0320 121 (helpline) or +44 (0) 28 9024 3249

Fax: 028 9023 5383

E-mail: hseni@detini.gov.uk

www.hseni.gov.uk

Health and safety guidance and advice is offered to those suffering workplace aggression and violence.

HR & Diversity Management Limited

PO Box 1276, Swindon SN25 4UX, UK

Tel: +44 (0) 845 22 55 787 (National Bullying Helpline)

E-mail: chris@hrdiversity.co.uk

www.hrdiversity.co.uk

HR & Diversity Management runs the National Bullying Helpline and the Bullying Business website.

International Labour Organization

SafeWork Programme, Geneva, Switzerland

Tel: +41 (0) 22 799 6715

Fax: +41 (0) 22 799 6878

E-mail: safework@ilo.org

www.ilo.org/public/english/protection/safework/stress/index.htm

A global programme on safety and health at work, offering guidance and advice.

International Stress Management Association UK

PO Box 26, South Petherton TA13 5WY, UK

Tel: +44 (0) 7000 780 430

E-mail:stress@isma.org.uk

www.isma.org.uk

ISMA exists to promote sound knowledge and best practice in the prevention and reduction of human stress. It sets professional standards for the benefit of individuals and organizations using the services of its members. There are links from website to other resources.

The Royal Society for the Prevention of Accidents (RoSPA)

RoSPA House, Edgbaston Park, 353 Bristol Road, Edgbaston, Birmingham B5 7ST, UK

Tel: +44 (0) 121 248 2000

Fax: +44 (0) 121 248 2001

E-mail: help@rospa.com

www.rospa.com

RoSPA offers guidance, advice and training for managers regarding stress and violence.

The Samaritans

10 The Grove, Slough, Berkshire SL1 1QP, UK

Or write to Chris, PO Box 9090, Stirling FK8 2SA

Tel: +44 (0) 175 353 2713 or 08457 90 90 90 (or check your local telephone directory for a local number)

Fax: +44 (0) 175 352 4332

E-mail: jo@samaritans.org

www.samaritans.org.uk

The Samaritans offer guidance and advice.

Sheffield Occupational Health Advisory Services (SOHAS)

3rd Floor, Queen's Buildings, 55 Queen Street, Sheffield S1 2DX, UK

Tel: +44 (0)114 275 5760

Fax: +44 (0) 114 249 1882

E-mail: sohas@sohas.co.uk

www.sohas.co.uk

SOHAS offers guidance and advice.

The Suzy Lamplugh Trust

14 East Sheen Avenue, London SW14 8AS, UK

Tel: +44 (0)181 392 1839

Fax: +44 (0)181 392 1830

E-mail:info@suzylamplugh.org

www.suzylamplugh.org

The Trust offers guidance and advice, particularly for those who work alone; it has DVDs for sale or hire.

Trades Union Congress (TUC)

Health and Safety Office, Congress House, 23 Great Russell Street, London WC1B 3LS, UK

Tel: +44 (0) 20 7636 4030

Fax: +44 (0) 20 7636 0632

www.tuc.org

The TUC offers health and safety guidance and advice to those suffering workplace aggression and violence.

Trauma After-Care Trust

Buttfields, The Farthings, Withington, Gloucestershire GL54 4DF, UK

Tel: +44 (0) 1242 890 306 (helpline) or +44 (0) 1242 890 498

Fax: +44 (0) 1242 890 498

E-mail: tact@tacthq.demon.co.uk

This is a charity to help people suffering from the psychological after-effects of trauma.

Traumatic Stress Service

Maudsley Hospital, Denmark Hill, Camberwell, London SE5 8AB, UK

Tel: +44 (0) 20 3228 2969

Fax: +44 (0) 20 3228 3573

E-mail: judith.erskine@slam.nhs.uk

www.slam.nhs.uk/services/pages/detail.asp?id=832

> This UK-wide service in counselling was initially linked with a range of major disasters, but the bulk of its work is now with lower-profile cases.

UK National Stress Network

9 Bell Lane, Syresham, Brackley NN13 5HP, UK

Tel: +44 (0) 7966 196033

Fax: +44 (0) 1280 850056

E-mail: iandraper@workstress.net

www.workstress.net

> An education and awareness raising campaign, offering guidance and advice.

Victim Support

National Office, Cranmer House, 39 Brixton Road,
London SW9 6DZ, UK

Tel: +44 (0) 845 30 30 900 (helpline) or +44 (0) 20 7735 9166

Fax: +44 (0) 20 7582 5712

E-mail: contact@victimsupport.org.uk

www.victimsupport.org.uk

> Victim Support is the national charity which helps crime victims. Its services are confidential and free.

Victim Support Northern Ireland

Annsgate House, 70–74 Ann Street, Belfast BT1 4EH

Tel: +44 (0) 123 224 4039

Fax: +44 (0) 123 231 3838

E-mail: info@victimsupportni.org.uk

Victim Support Scotland

15/23 Hardwell Close, Edinburgh EH8 9RX, UK

Tel: +44 (0) 131 668 4486

Fax: +44 (0) 131 662 5400

E-mail: info@victimsupportsco.demon.co.uk

Victim Support Wales

146 Whitchurch Road, Cardiff CF14 3NA, UK

Tel: +44 (0) 2920 61 43 00

Fax :+44 (0)2920 61 71 41

E-mail: jon.trew@victimsupportwales.org.uk

Workplace Health Connect

Tel: +44 (0) 845 609 6006

www.workplacehealthconnect.co.uk

This is a free service for the managers and staff of small and medium-sized enterprises that provides practical advice on workplace health and safety.

Appendix D
Legislation

Health and safety law applies to risks from violence, just as it does to other risks from work. The main pieces of relevant legislation that will be of interest are:

The Employment Act 2002 (Dispute Resolution) Regulations 2004 SI 2004 No. 752

After coming into force on 1 October 2004, these regulations have set new rules which all employers have to follow in dispute resolution. See www.opsi.gov.uk/si/si2004/20040752.htm.

The Employment Equality (Age) Regulations 2006 SI No. 2006 No. 1031

Having come into force on 1 October 2006, these cover age discrimination. For the regulations, see www.opsi.gov.uk/si/si2006/20061031.htm and for an explanatory memorandum see www.opsi.gov.uk/si/em2006/uksiem_20061031_en.pdf (143 pages).

The Employment Equality (Age) (Amendment) Regulations 2006, SI 2006 No. 2408

These came into force on 30 September 2006. See www.opsi.gov.uk/si/si2006/20062408.htm.

The Employment Equality (Age) (Amendment No. 2) Regulations 2006, SI No. 2931

In force since 1 December 2006, these regulations are available at www.opsi.gov.uk/si/si2006/20062931.htm and an explanatory memorandum can be found at www.opsi.gov.uk/si/em2006/uksiem_20062931_en.pdf (10 pages).

The Employment Equality (Sex Discrimination) Regulations 2005 SI 2005 No. 2467

Under this piece of legislation, any form of harassment is unlawful. See www.opsi.gov.uk/si/si2005/20052467.htm.

Employment Rights Act 1996

The parts dealing with unfair dismissal, constructive dismissal and victimization are particularly relevant. See www.opsi.gov.uk/acts/acts1996/1996018.htm, or to obtain full text copies or order go to www.opsi.gov.uk.

The Health and Safety at Work etc. Act 1974 (HSW Act)

Employers have a legal duty under this Act to ensure, as far as reasonably practicable, the health, safety and welfare at work of their employees. This legislation is not available on the OPSI website.

Human Rights Act 1998

The Act came into force on 2 October 2000. It incorporates and brings into force the provisions of the European Convention on Human Rights. See www.opsi.gov.uk/acts/acts1998/19980042.htm.

The Management of Health and Safety at Work Regulations 1999 SI 1999 No. 3242

Employers must consider the risks to employees (including the risk of reasonably foreseeable stress and violence), decide how significant these risks are, decide what to do to prevent or control the risks and develop a clear management plan to achieve this. See www.legislation.hmso.gov.uk/si/si1999/19993242.htm.

The Management of Health and Safety at Work (Amendment) Regulations 2006 SI 2006 No. 438

See www.opsi.gov.uk/si/si2006/20060438.htm for the actual legislation and www.opsi.gov.uk/si/em2006/uksiem_20060438_en.pdf for an explanatory memorandum.

The Protection from Harassment Act 1997

This Act makes provision for protecting persons from harassment and similar conduct. A person must not pursue a course of conduct which amounts to harassment of another, and which he/she knows or ought to know amounts to harassment of the others. See www.opsi.gov.uk/acts/acts1997/1997040.htm.

The Reporting of Injuries, Diseases and Dangerous Occurrences Regulations 1995 (RIDDOR) SI 1995 No. 3163

Employers must notify their enforcing authority in the event of an accident at work of any employee resulting in death, major injury or incapacity for normal work for three or more days. This includes any act of physical violence done to a person at work. See www.opsi.gov.uk/si/si1995/uksi_19953163_en_1.htm.

Safety Representatives and Safety Committees Regulations 1977 (a) and The Health and Safety (Consultation with Employees) Regulations 1996 (b) SI 1977 No. 500

Employers must inform, and consult with, employees in good time on matters relating to their health and safety. Employee representatives, either appointed by recognized trade unions under (a) or elected under (b), may make representations to their employer on matters affecting the health and safety of those they represent. These regulations are not available on the OPSI website.

Index

Setting Up a Library and Information Service from Scratch
Sheila Pantry OBE and Peter Griffiths

'*I found the book useful, easy-to-read, and would recommend it to those already running library and information services as well as to those just starting out.*'   FreePint

This eminently practical guide is written to help all those who need to set up a library and information service within their organization, irrespective of subject background or type of organization. It offers support to people who have qualifications but no experience in setting up such a service, and those who have had no training at all. Both authors have had many years' experience of setting up information services for a wide range of organizations in the UK and many other countries.

The book will hold your hand as you tackle the many tasks and responsibilities needed to create a successful library and information service – irrespective of size – and takes you step by step through the processes involved, including:

- the reasons for setting up a library and information service
- first steps: the information audit
- meeting the information needs of specialists
- establishing the library: premises, design and technical requirements
- staffing: recruitment and management
- managing budgets and finance
- networking and locating sources of information
- acquisition, organization and dissemination: print and electronic
- services to be provided by the library
- sources of support for the library inside and outside the organization
- promotion of the library
- training staff and users.

This is a vital guide for anyone, whether an information professional or not, facing the challenge of setting up a library and information service from scratch.

2005; 208pp; paperback; 978-1-85604-558-2; £34.95

Your Essential Guide to Career Success
Sheila Pantry OBE and Peter Griffiths

Second edition

'An essential read for anyone looking for a first career job in library or information science, and also for the more seasoned veteran looking to take the next step.'　　　　　　　　　　　　　　　　　　　New Library World

'…upbeat, easy to read, brief and full of encouraging ideas and examples.'　　　　　　　　　　　　　　　　　　　Marketing Library Services

'It is the sort of book which managers should have on their bookshelf in order to help those they manage.'　　　　　　　　　　　Managing Information

How ambitious are you? Do you have a career plan? Are your skills up-to-date? Where do you want to be in three, five or ten years' time? This book is an essential read for any information professional eager to prosper in the global library and information environment of the 21st century. Whether you are a new entrant to the profession wishing to know how to get a foot on the ladder, an information professional in mid-career wishing to progress, or a candidate for a more senior position needing a view of the current state of the profession, it offers guidance on managing every stage of your career, including:

- meeeting the challenges of today's employment market
- your master career plan
- starting your career: areas of work for LIS professionals
- applying for a job
- next steps in your career: developing a job promotion plan
- your successful interview
- after the interview
- looking sideways: alternative career strategies.

This is an essential deskbook to explore if you are an information professional in any sector and at any level wishing to learn the skills and techniques to sell yourself with confidence to current and future employers.

2003; 208pp; paperback; 978-1-85604-491-2; £22.95

CILIP: taking you where you want to be

Is job satisfaction important to you? Would you like greater recognition within your organisation? Are you hoping to progress up the career ladder?

If your answer is yes to one or more of these questions CILIP can help.

We believe that job satisfaction comes from doing a job to the best of your ability and from getting recognition from your manager, your colleagues and your customers.

By investing in CILIP membership you can benefit from a range of services, including new online content, which will help you do your job better and enhance your career prospects.

For your free membership pack, email findoutmore@cilip.org.uk today.

Chartered Institute of
Library and Information
Professionals

www.cilip.org.uk/member
Now even more reasons to belong

CILIP: training & development
training you can trust

CILIP Training & Development provides the widest range of training for the LIS community in the UK. With over 120 one and two-day courses running annually on around 90 different topics, our training caters for all sectors and levels of experience. All our courses are tailored to meet the learning, training and developmental needs of the modern library and information community.

Why train with CILIP?

- 98% of participants rate our courses as "Good to Excellent"
- Experienced and expert facilitators
- Purpose built training rooms
- Limited number of participants to ensure highly participative and interactive events
- Comprehensive training materials
- Hot buffet lunch with every full day course

www.cilip.org.uk/trainingcourses